Artist-Craftsman **Carl E. Paak** is professor of art in the Fine Arts Department of the University of New Mexico in Albuquerque. He has encouraged ceramic students to use many and varied approaches to clay form and surface decoration in the attempt to integrate a personal attitude toward the creation of the clay object as an art form.

He has worked in all ranges of firing temperatures, using gas and electric kilns with earthenware, stoneware, and porcelain clays.

His work has been exhibited nationally in ceramic and sculpture exhibits, as well as in many regional shows over the past 25 years.

Mr. Paak is an active member of the American Craft Council, the World Crafts Council, and local affiliates.

BOOKS IN THE CREATIVE HANDCRAFTS SERIES

Carl E. Paak

THE DECORATIVE TOUCH

HOW TO DECORATE, GLAZE, AND FIRE YOUR POTS

A SPECTRUM BOOK

PRENTICE-HALL, INC., ENGLEWOOD CLIFFS, NEW JERSEY 07632

Library of Congress Cataloging in Publication Data

Paak, Carl E
  The decorative touch.

  (A Spectrum Book) (The Creative Handcrafts
Series)
  Bibliography: p.
  Includes index.
  1. Pottery craft. I. Title.
TT920.P22   738.1'5   80-29173
ISBN 0-13-198085-8
ISBN 0-13-198077-7 (pbk.)

Editorial production/supervision and interior design
  by *Heath Lynn Silberfeld*
Cover design by *Michael Freeland*
Insert design by *Christine Gehring Wolf*
Manufacturing buyer: *Cathie Lenard*

10 9 8 7 6 5 4 3 2 1

Printed in the United States of America

PRENTICE-HALL INTERNATIONAL, INC., *London*
PRENTICE-HALL OF AUSTRALIA PTY. LIMITED, *Sydney*
PRENTICE-HALL OF CANADA, LTD., *Toronto*
PRENTICE-HALL OF INDIA PRIVATE LIMITED, *New Delhi*
PRENTICE-HALL OF JAPAN, INC., *Tokyo*
PRENTICE-HALL OF SOUTHEAST ASIA PTE. LTD., *Singapore*
WHITEHALL BOOKS LIMITED, *Wellington, New Zealand*

Contents

Lawrence Lucas. *Goat Dog*. Heavily grogged clay built on a brick armature. Bisque-fired, then Raku-fired with glass red glaze and white crackle glaze. Height 18″, length 14″.

Preface

This book is written to give the beginning potter insight into the methods and materials normally used to decorate, glaze, and fire clay forms. Techniques will be described, and emphasis will be placed on what *not* to do at various stages of completing the clay objects.

Through reading this book, it is hoped, the potter will learn to prevent accidents and to eliminate many unnecessary problems, although it is true that one learns from mistakes. This will result in positive reinforcement and personal satisfaction because the success of the completed clay form allows the beginning potter to progress toward a greater sense of accomplishment.

The techniques described in this book will acquaint the reader with methods of applying decoration. The photographs will expand the various ways in which the contemporary ceramic artist can interpret and use these techniques for his or her own personal expression of clay form and decoration. The blend—the enhancement of decoration with the clay form—is the ultimate goal of the potter whether the final product be utilitarian or a sculptural shape.

It is only through practice and self-analysis that the beginning potter can become an individual in the use of clay and decoration to express personal ideas.

Throughout the 5,000 years of humanity's development of visual and tactile expression in clay, each civilization has interpreted ideas in a different way. The methods of decoration have not greatly changed. It is hoped that the reader will become aware of the many books that present a historical and contemporary overview, in photographs, of how people as potters and ceramic artists have contributed to the varied ways of expressing the times in which they have lived.

In a brief historical overview, we find that early humans, as individual artists, were unknown, but their work has survived to give us insight into the strengths of the period. The early Jōmon and Haniwa periods of Japan gave us great, robust, hand-built slab forms that resulted in beautiful integration of form and decoration. Greek pottery, with its severe form and limited shapes, gave us a story-telling clay surface. The vessel became a three-dimensional surface upon which to express the sensitive linear drawings of Greek life and sport. The Chinese Tang dynasty was a period of noble clay sculpture, with the magnificant Tang horses ranging from small to full-scale in size. Here, form overshadowed any surface decoration. Classical proportion of form, as we know it today, came from the Chinese Sung dynasty. Rich glazes were developed and used to enhance the shape. The visual relationship of parts of the thrown forms were of utmost importance.

The strong Incan pots of Peru combined function with form and surface decoration. The intricate patterns of Islamic tile work gave a rich wall-surface decoration to exquisite buildings such as the Alhambra. The use of brushwork as a calligraphic design is found in all parts of the world from the luster plates of Hispano-Moresque design to the sensitive brush work of Hamada and Kawai in Japan. This use of the brush as the main element of design becomes an integral part of the clay surface. Form and decoration become one in total concept.

On the contemporary scene, Peter Voulkos has done more to break the past traditions of clay form than any single person working in clay. With the background of a "formal potter" in the early 1950s, Voulkos burst through the then-accepted traditions of clay form in a forceful and exciting variety of clay ideas. The ceramic artist as an individual now injects his or her personal feelings into clay and shows a diversity of approaches for creating finished clay objects.

The clay form changes, but the techniques, the tools, and the methods of decoration applied to these clay pieces vary little. This book discusses techniques which, after being tried and learned, can assist the individual potter with his or her own personal expression.

We will discuss what happens if (1) you apply too thin or too thick a coat of glaze; (2) you apply oxides under the glaze; (3) you apply oxides too thickly over a glaze; (4) you leave glaze on the bottom of a pot; (5) you don't kiln-wash the shelves; (6) you fire greenware too fast; (7) you open a glaze kiln before it has cooled sufficiently. We will also discuss the advisability of kiln sitters on an electric kiln and the constant need for testing new glazes.

These and other problems are a common part of working with the clay form and will be introduced in each chapter as they apply to a specific need for the potter adding his or her finished touch to the clay object.

I wish to express my gratitude and appreciation to the many ceramic artists and friends who have helped with their time and knowledge in preparation of this book. For personal encouragement: my wife, Elizabeth. For reading my manuscript: Professor Emeritus Glenn Nelson, Ceramics, University of Minnesota, Duluth, Minnesota; Associate Professor Joe Bova, Ceramics, Louisiana State University, Baton Rouge. For the excellent black-and-white photographs throughout the book: J. Fredrick Laval, Albuquerque, New Mexico. For submitting slides of their work: the many ceramic artists, both student and professional, whose works show the varied approaches to creating a ceramic form.

THE
DECORATIVE
TOUCH

Author. Three vases. Wheel-thrown red stoneware. Clay added around neck from forms trimmed directly after throwing. Added clay waxed. Top portions of vases dipped in white mat glaze, lower sections in brown glaze, center unglazed. Gas reduction firing C/9.

1

Decorating Techniques on Greenware

MAKING CLAY SLIPS

One of the oldest methods of decoration known to man is the application of a clay slip of contrasting color to the surface of a pot. The method has not changed, but the decorating techniques and designs have varied with different cultures through the ages and have expanded with the creativity of the individual potter.

Slip is clay in liquid suspension. The consistency of the clay slip can be thick or thin depending on the amount of water used with the powdered clay (Fig. 1-1). When making a clay slip, fill a plastic container half full with water and add dry clay to the water until the container is full. Allow the dry clay to saturate into the water thoroughly before mixing the two. If the slip is too thin, permit it to stand overnight and pour off the excess water. If it is too thick, add water to give the slip a consistency that will allow it to be brushed on the clay surface without dripping.

Slip decoration allows the potter to change the body color; for example, white slip may be used over a red clay body or red slip

1-1. Author. *Winter Snow-scape.*
Rounded porcelain clay slab. Thick
porcelain slip applied to damp ware.
Forced drying allows slip to crack.
Crackle glaze applied overall. After
firing, black india ink brushed over slip
cracks. Electric firing C/6. Length 16″.

over a white clay body. The slip usually should be of the same
firing range as the clay body (Fig. 1-2). This will ensure equal
shrinkage of the slip with the clay form (Fig. 1-3). If you are using
an earthenware low-fire clay body, use an earthenware slip; if you
are using a stoneware body, use a stoneware slip. *All natural clay
slips must be applied only to a wet or damp greenware clay form and
allowed to dry slowly with the pot (Fig. 1-4). If the slip is applied to dry
greenware, the pot will absorb moisture from the slip too quickly, and the
slip will flake off the pot.*

1-2. Author. Stoneware covered jar.
Stoneware slip with silicon carbide
mixed in to produce crater effect.
Height 10″, width 8″.

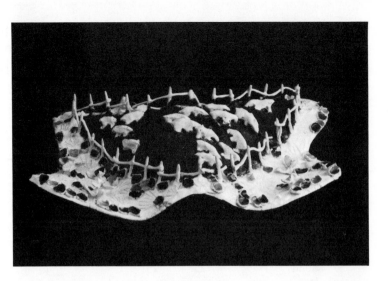

1-3. Author. *Sheep-scape.* Slab porcelain form. Center dark area covered with thick porcelain slip with granular manganese dioxide for color. Underglazes brushed on greenware. Mat white glaze overall. Electric firing C/6. Diameter 14".

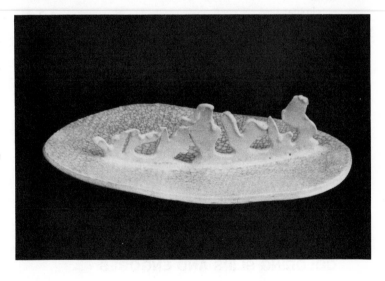

1-4. Author. *Winter Tree-scape.* Low porcelain slab. Tree forms cut out of porcelain and adhered to slab. Thick porcelain white slip applied over top of tree forms. Crackle glaze overall. Base shape brushed with black india ink after glaze firing, then wiped off to accent crackle. Electric firing C/6. Diameter 14".

MAKING CLAY ENGOBES

An *engobe* is a white clay slip with added fluxes or calcined materials. But the change in composition allows application on dry greenware, damp greenware, or bisqueware. Engobes for dry greenware cannot be used on damp ware or bisqueware and vice versa.

Table 1-1 lists various engobe formulas and their temperature ranges. Coloring oxides can be added to any formula.

Reading vertically, each column headed Damp, Dry, or Bisque adds up to 100 grams. For an example, if you want to make 600 grams of any engobe, multiply the listed amount of each material by 6 and weigh the batch.

TABLE 1-1 ENGOBE COMPOSITIONS CHART

	CONE 08 to 2			CONE 3 to 6			CONE 7 to 12		
	Damp	Dry	Bisque	Damp	Dry	Bisque	Damp	Dry	Bisque
Kaolin	20	15	5	20	15	5	20	15	5
Ball clay	25	15	15	25	15	15	25	15	15
Leadless frit	20	10	10		5	5			5
Calcined kaolin		25	25	15	20			15	15
Soda feldspar					5	5	25	20	20
Nepheline syenite				20	10	15			10
Talc	5	5	15	5	5	5			
Flint	15	15	15	15	15	15	15	20	15
Borax	5	5	5	5	5	5	5	5	5
Zircopax, Ultrox, Superpax	10	10	10	10	10	10	10	10	10
	100 gram	100 gram	100 gram	100 gram	100 gram	100 gram	100 gram	100 gram	100 gram

COLORING SLIPS AND ENGOBES

To color slips and engobes it is necessary to start with a white clay body in powder form if an accurate and repeatable color is desired (Fig. 1-5). The slip or engobe is weighed. About 600 grams will fill a 1-pound plastic container after water is added. The percentage of oxide color is always multiplied by the total dry weight of the slip or engobe to determine the amount of oxide to use. The dry oxide color is then mixed well with the dry-base slip. Fill the plastic container about half full with water and add slip to the water, letting the dry clay slake thoroughly before stirring to avoid dry lumps of clay from forming in the wet mixture (Figs. 1-6 through 1-9). Allow at least 1 hour for the slip to soak into the water.

1-5. Author. Low porcelain-slab form. Light blue porcelain slip over basic form. Thin, torn porcelain shapes laid over blue slip. Very slow drying. White mat glaze overall. Electric firing C/8. Diameter 14".

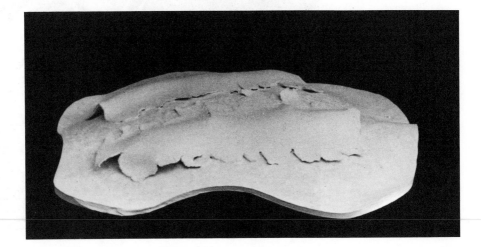

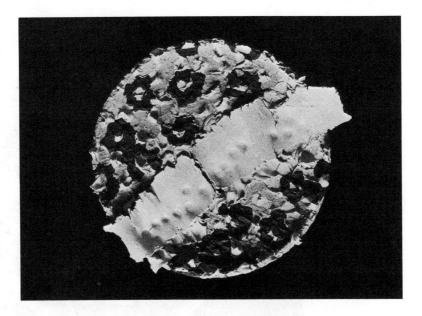

1-6. Author. *Moon Walk*. Wheel-thrown low bowl. White stoneware clay covered with very thick porcelain and earthenware slips with silicon carbide. Thin, torn porcelain slab laid over slip. Very slow drying. White mat glaze overall. Heavy melting of earthenware slips. Strong textures. Electric firing C/8. Diameter 16".

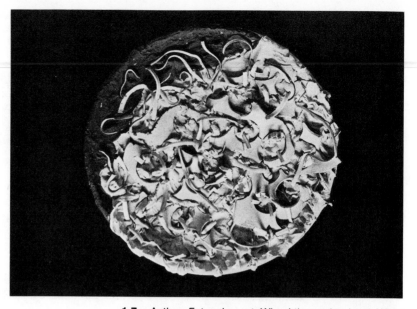

1-7. Author. *Entanglement*. Wheel-thrown low bowl. White stoneware clay. Very thick porcelain and red earthenware slip with silicon carbide. Porcelain trimmings imbedded in wet slip. Transparent glaze overall. High textural surface. Very slow drying. Electric firing C/8. Diameter 15″.

1.8. Author. *Eruption*. Wheel-thrown low bowl. White stoneware clay. Technique similar to 1-6 and 1-7. Electric firing C/8. Diameter 14″.

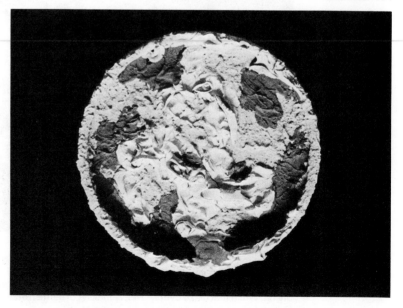

1-9. Author. *Mountains and Shadows.* Similar to 1-6, 1-7, and 1-8. Vanadium stain added to thick porcelain slip with silicon carbide to produce a yellow-tan color under a transparent glaze. Burnt umber brushed over peaks of slip for dark brown accent. Electric firing C/8. Diameter 14″.

Chart of Oxides for Slips:

6% Iron oxide	Light tan
10% Iron oxide	Brown
14% Iron oxide	Dark brown
2% Cobalt oxide	Blue
2% Cobalt carbonate	Blue
2% Black copper oxide	Green
5% Copper carbonate	Green
6% Manganese dioxide	Purple-brown
10% Rutile	Tan
3% Iron oxide 2% Cobalt oxide 4% Manganese dioxide	Black
2% Cobalt oxide 4% Iron oxide	Gray-blue

Keep all the trimmings and scrap white clay you accumulate (Fig. 1-10). Let them dry out thoroughly, then crush the clay into small particles using a rolling pin or hammer. Fill a gallon container half full of water and put the crushed clay into the water, filling the container. Label the jars as to the date the contents were soaked and let them sit without stirring from 1 to 4 weeks. Keep the container tightly covered. And, do not worry if a green mold covers the clay slip! Mold breaks down the clay particles and produces a more plastic slip.

1-10. Porcelain trimmings. To be dried, crushed, and soaked for slip.

If oxide colors are added to an already wet white slip, the color is only an approximation and cannot be repeated from batch to batch. When adding oxides to a wet slip, add a little water to the oxide, stirring it into solution before adding the oxide to the wet slip. This allows the oxide to mix better with the wet slip.

Low-fire earthenware slip can be applied to a damp stoneware body (Fig. 1-11A,B). *Because of the differences in shrinkage, slow, careful drying will allow the low-fire slip to adhere to the body.* Additions of about 10% silicon carbide (60 mesh) to the slip will produce a volcanic melted-slip surface when the clay form is fired between

C/4 (2167°F) and C/6 (2232°F) in either electric or gas-reduction firing. Silicon carbide added to any slip or engobe will break through a glaze texture. A mat glaze works best over the slip because the stiff, drier glaze surface retains the roughness of this slip (Figs. 1-12, 1-13, A,B).

1-11A. Author. Wheel-thrown porcelain vase. Thick earthenware slip with silicon carbide, mat glaze. Slip melted and cratered through the glaze. Gas reduction firing C/9. Height 12".

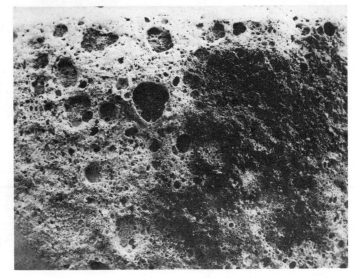

1-11B. Close-up of 1-11A.

1-12. Author. *Winter Hill*-scape. Porcelain slab covered with porcelain slip and silicon carbide (60-mesh) for rough texture. Trees added. Crackle glaze overall. Electric firing C/6. Diameter 12″.

1-13A. Author. Three wheel vases thrown off-center. Thick porcelain slip with silicon carbide (60-mesh) glazed with a tan mat. Cratering but no melting because porcelain slip is a high-temperature clay. Gas reduction firing C/9. Height 10″.

1-13B. Close-up of 1-13A.

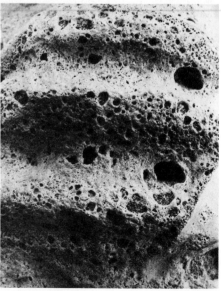

DECORATING CLAY IN THE PLASTIC STATE

As soon as the clay form has stiffened enough to retain its shape, colored clays can be added to the surface as a relief decoration or inserted into a cutout section of the body of the form. The consistency of the added colored clay should be similar to that of the body to which it is added.

There are several methods of introducing coloring oxides into clay: (1) Using a white clay, the same as the clay form, add small amounts of oxide powder to the clay (Fig. 1-14). Knead the oxide into the clay with your fingers, then apply or insert the colored clay into the body of the form. This method will give a variegated color surface which, when glazed with a translucent, white, or transparent glaze, will show the colored clay through the glaze. (2) Take a white slip, add oxide to the slip, pour the slip on a plaster bat, and allow the slip to stiffen. Then apply the colored clay to the surface

1-14. Joan Weissman. Slab-formed vase of porcelain clay. Cut-out slab. Colored clays laid together, then back of slab filled with white porcelain. All slabs put together to form the vase. After bisque firing, a thin wash of cobalt oxide sponged over the surface, then wiped off, leaving a thin blue line of color where colored clays connect and in five sgraffito line patterns cut into the colored clays. Colored clay area unglazed. Transparent glaze over rest of form. Electric firing C/9. Height 11½".

or insert it into the cutout areas. Dry slowly. When glazed with a translucent, white, or transparent glaze, the colored clay will show through the glaze as a solid color. (3) Marbleizing is another method of getting a color variation by wedging together a white and any other colored clay body of the same maturing temperature. This type of color variation can be very effective in either wheel-thrown or slab-built forms. *Do not wedge the clays too much or the intermix will be too weak and leave no color pattern.* If the surface of the marbleized clay becomes obscured or smudged, scrape the surface to reveal the color contrast after the clay has become leather-hard.

DECORATING CLAY IN THE LEATHER-HARD STATE

At this stage the clay form has stiffened; however the pot still has enough moisture to allow for the following methods of decorating the greenware.

1. SGRAFFITO

Sgraffito decoration is a process of cutting through a contrasting colored slip or engobe to expose the clay body (Fig. 1-15). Slip is applied to the damp greenware and allowed to dry partially. The

1-15. Lissa Paak. Vase. Slab-built red stoneware with white stoneware slip. Design cut through white slip. No glaze. Gas reduction firing C/9. Height 10".

entire surface can be brushed or dipped, or sections of the pot can be painted in a design pattern. Slip or engobe should be applied thickly enough so the clay body beneath does not show through the contrasting liquid clay coat. *Do not allow the slip to dry thoroughly; otherwise it may flake off as you cut into the clay surface.* Large or small areas of applied slip can be scraped off and linear patterns can be incised through the slip to reveal the contrasting clay body (Fig. 1-16). Do not brush off the rough edges until the slip is completely dry or the pattern will be smudged. *This is especially true if a fine linear pattern is cut into the slip.* Always allow slip to dry slowly. Cover the pot to prevent direct air drying. If the slip dries while the pot form is still damp, this unequal drying might cause the slip to peel off the clay form. *This slow drying is necessary for all decorative methods used on damp greenware.*

1-16. Author. Wheel-thrown porcelain bottle. Thick porcelain clip with mine tailings. Sgraffito pattern cut through wet slip. Mat tan glaze overall. Gas reduction firing C/9. Height 12".

2. SLIP TRAILING

This is a method of applying a raised line of slip or engobe on the damp pot surface (Fig. 1-17). Use a plastic ketchup or mustard container or an ear syringe, filling the container with a *thick slip. The slip should not be thin or the line pattern will not stay raised. The pot should be damper than usual.*

Use a spray bottle with water and dampen the surface of the ware, then allow moisture to penetrate the clay surface before trailing a slip pattern. *Dry very slowly or the raised line will flake off the pot.* Slip trailing is a spontaneous method of decoration. It is necessary to keep the slip container moving or the liquid clay will pile up in a glob on the surface. To get the feel of slip trailing, try trailed patterns on a damp slab of clay.

3. SLIP COMBING

This is a variation of slip trailing. A series of parallel slip-trailed lines are laid on the damp ware close together. A fine feather is dragged across the raised slip lines at a right angle to the line

1-17. Author. Covered jar. Wheel-thrown red stoneware. Slip trailing with red stoneware slip, 5% manganese dioxide added to darken slip. Gas reduction firing C/9. Diameter 10".

pattern, creating a delicate, broken linear movement. A pointed tool made of wood or a fork can also be dragged through the linear slip pattern (Fig. 1-18). If the surface is flat enough, a coarse comb could be brought across the wet slip lines. Constrasting slip or engobe colors give a stronger visual linear pattern. Dry slowly.

1-18. Author. Wheel-thrown red stoneware bowl. Thick white engobe applied to bowl with a syringe. Fine feather dragged across slip to create broken line. Transparent glaze applied overall. Gas reduction firing C/9. Diameter 8″.

4. MISHIMA INLAY

Mishima is a Korean term for putting a contrasting color in a line. The process will also be described when glazes are discussed. A linear pattern is incised into the damp clay surface (Fig. 1-19A). A contrasting color of slip or engobe is quickly brushed into the incised line. When the slip has dried slightly, the surface is scraped clean of slip, leaving the slip in the incised lines (Fig. 1-19B). This decorating technique works best if a strong line is cut into the clay. Dry the pot slowly.

1-19A. Author. Wheel-thrown red stoneware vase. Mishima decoration in center. Linear sgraffito design cut into damp greenware. Lines filled with porcelain slip with iron oxide. Surface scraped. Tan mat glaze applied. Gas reduction firing C/9. Height 10″.

1-19B. Close-up of 1-19A.

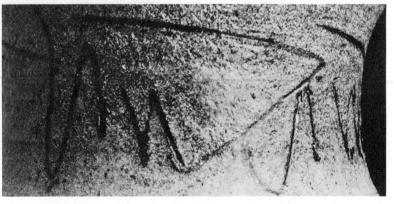

5. ADDED CLAY

Addition of clay to the surface of the damp pot offers a great possibility for embellishment of the clay form (Fig. 1-20). Clay added to a damp body usually works best if it is composed of *the same clay as the pot form* (Figs. 1-21 A,B). Slip used to adhere the added clay form should also be made from the same clay as the

16

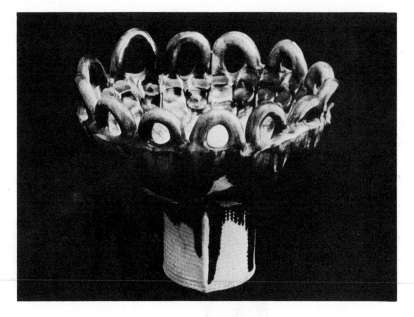

1-20. Author. One-piece, white stoneware, slab-form planter with added slab foot and added clay coils on rim. Transparent glaze with dark-green glaze overlap. Gas reduction firing C/9. Diameter 10″.

1-21A. Author. Covered jar. Wheel-thrown. Added clay figures and textured body. One dark glaze overall. Small areas waxed and left unglazed. Unglazed areas painted with gold model-car enamel after firing. Gas reduction firing C/9. Height 10″.

1-21B. Close-up of 1-21A.

body (Fig. 1-22). By using the same clay for the pot, the slip, and the added clay forms, shrinkage is equalized in drying and firing and the chance of the added clay cracking off from the pot is reduced (Fig. 1-23). Clay coils, strips, cutouts, handles, knobs, or free forms may be added to the pot (Fig. 1-24). Before adding clay, crosshatch the surface of the pot, coat both surfaces with thick slip, and adhere the shape with a firm, steady pressure (Fig. 1-25). Since the added clay is always softer than the pot form, slow drying is always

1-22. Author. Wheel-thrown vase. Clay slabs added on surface. One glaze overall. Color variation due to change in glaze thickness. Gas reduction firing C/9. Height 14″.

1-23. Author. Wheel-thrown bowl. Figures added to rim. Single glaze overall. Gas reduction firing C/9. Diameter 12″.

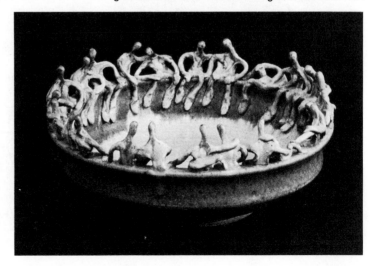

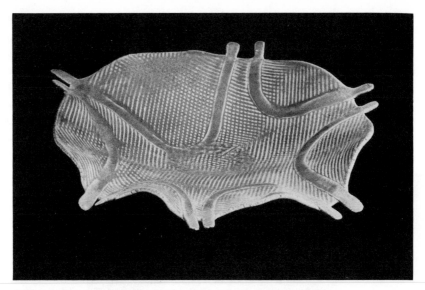

1-24. Author. Low bowl. Single porcelain slab construction with thin slab overlay rolled into slab base. Single mat glaze overall. Gas reduction C/9. Diameter 12″.

1-25. Author. *Everbloom*. Wheel-thrown red stoneware. Added clay unglazed. Blue glaze on base. Added clay waxed to keep glaze off surfaces. Areas painted red and white with model-car enamels after firing. Gas reduction firing C/9. Height 15″.

necessary to equalize the moisture of the pot and added clay (Figs. 1-26A,B and 1-27 to 1-29). At times added precautions must be taken in drying. Handles which spring from the pot are especially prone to cracking along the curve and at the upper attachment of the handle. When the handle starts to dry, wax the joints where they are attached to the pot to prevent the clay body from drying too fast. The wax used is a commercial, water-base wax emulsion

1-26A. Author. *Under the Rainbow.* Porcelain slab construction with added figures. Crackle glaze overall. All surfaces sponged with black india ink and washed off to bring out crackle lines. Electric firing C/6. Height 15".

1-26B. Close-up of 1-26A.

which can be purchased at any ceramic supply outlet. Dilute the wax emulsion with one-half the amount of water. The thin wax emulsion is easier to apply and it dries faster. This waxing of added clay, regardless of form, prevents a lot of problems, such as the tendency of the added clay to pull away from the body of the pot. Another method of preventing the handles from drying too fast is to wrap them with flexible plastic.

1-27. Mexico. Slab construction. Low-fire clay covered with white slip. Added clay also covered with white slip. Banded decoration applied with thin mixture of red slip. Firing around C/04. Height 7".

1-28. Mexico. *Tree of Life.* Coil-constructed low-fire clay. Clay added by attaching wire to clay shapes and imbedding wire into basic tree form. Technique can only be used in low-temperature firing around C/06 to C/04. The clay does not shrink much, and the wire does not melt. Height 7".

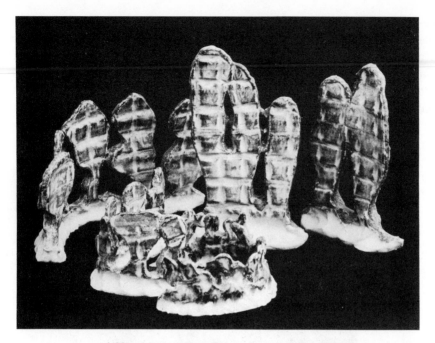

1-29. Author. *Winter Grove*. A group of five separate tree forms. Slabs of porcelain rolled with textured roller. Trees cut out and placed vertically in different relationships. Black underglaze brushed over the greenware, dried, and fired. Transparent glaze used overall. Electric firing C/6. Diameter of group 18".

6. STAMPING

Stamping an impression into a clay form or stamping out shapes to be added to the pot is another variation of surface decoration. Stamping a pattern into the pot surface requires greater moisture control of the clay form (Figs. 1-30A,B, 1-31). If the pot is too stiff, attempts to stamp a decoration into the surface will crack the clay. A softer surface will respond to pressure. The surface must not be wet or the stamp shape will stick to the pot and the impression will not be clear (Fig. 1-32). Clay stamps can easily be made and bisque-fired before using (Fig. 1-33). Cut away the background of the stamp, leaving a high relief which will easily penetrate the pot surface without too much pressure.

There is an endless array of forms which will produce an impression in the soft clay. Shells, sticks, fingers, pencils, tubes, etc., can create positive or negative patterns. Clay can be added to parts of the pot, then stamped, or clay shapes can be stamped out and then

1-30A. Author. Slab platter. Single heavy slab construction. Red stoneware. Overlay of slab strips. Stamped impressions on surface. White and brown mat glazes poured overall. Iron oxide brushed over glaze. Gas reduction firing C/9. Diameter 15″.

1-30B. Close-up of 1-30A.

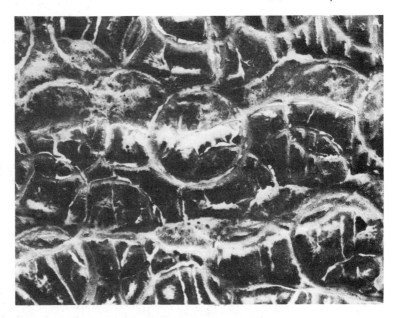

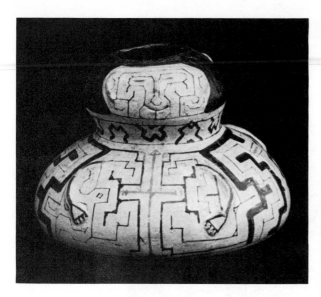

1-31. Shipapu Indians from the Peruvian jungle. Low-fire clay, coil-built with very thin walls. Covered with white slip. Fine line decoration applied with contrasting slip. Fired around C/08 to C/06. Surface shellacked after firing. Height 8″.

1-32. Author. Wheel-thrown red stoneware vase. Center head pressed from a one-piece, Pre-Columbian clay mold from Ecuador. Gas reduction firing C/9. Height 14″.

1-33. Author. Bisque-fired clay stamps can be used to create a variety of motifs for individual or repetitive patterns in damp greenware. Diameter 1″.

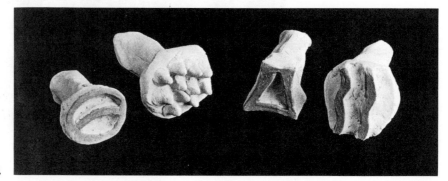

added to the clay form. This added clay will give a high-relief pattern on the clay surface. Adhere all added clay with thick slip and dry the form slowly.

7. INCISING AND EXCISING CLAY

Incising a design into the moist clay produces a negative linear pattern. The depth of the carving depends on the thickness of the wall of the pot. In reverse, *excising* or *relief carving* creates a low-relief design in which the background is cut away, allowing the design to project from the surface of the pot. The depth of this relief depends on the thickness of the wall of the pot. In both types of carving into the clay, lightly draw your design on the clay surface before cutting.

8. PIERCING

Piercing the clay surface requires a controlled moisture of the clay body (Fig. 1-34). A fettling knife is a good tool for this process because the narrow tip of the knife gives less surface contact with the clay and allows the knife to cut more easily through the clay. *If the knife does not cut easily into the clay, do not try piercing the pot, as the*

1-34. Peru. Church. Unglazed, slab built. Contrasting white and brown clay slips for decoration. Firing about C/06 to C/04. Height 16".

body will crack. Any rough edges left from cutting out the clay can gently be sponged off. Use a damp, not wet, sponge, as you do not want to wet the clay surface after piercing the form. Allow for very slow drying after piercing is finished.

9. BURNISHING

This decoration procedure is a method of giving the clay a shiny surface (Fig. 1-35). A smooth stone, the back of a spoon, or a flat piece of wood can be used to polish the clay surface in the leather-hard state. Burnished pots are never fired at bisque temperatures above C/06 (1830°F) or the surface will dull and the sheen will disappear. This process works well with Raku firing, described in Chapter 8.

1-35. Rick Dillingham. Raku bottle. Slab-constructed in a sling. Damp greenware surface burnished, fired, and lightly reduced. Raku-fired about C/08. Diameter 16".

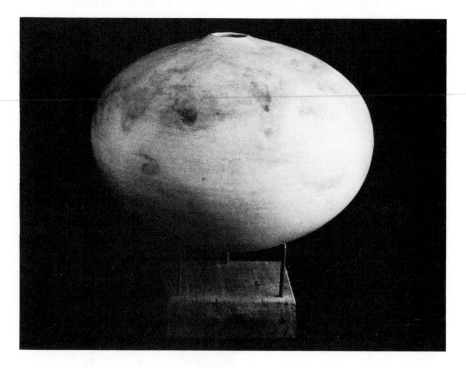

10. WAX RESIST

These designs can be readily applied on damp ware in combination with a slip, oxide colors, or liquid underglaze colors (Fig. 1-36). *Use a soft brush when applying the wax. When finished, wash the brush in soap and water. Do not let wax harden in the brush because it is very hard to dissolve the wax completely once hardened. If the wax does harden in the brush, use ammonia or alcohol to soften it.*

1-36. Author. Covered jar. Wheel-thrown white stoneware. Wax resist on greenware. Dark brown slip brushed over surface, transparent glaze overall. Gas reduction firing C/9. Height 7".

Brushing wax designs on damp greenware to create a color contrast generally works best on a white body (Fig. 1-37A,B). The wax design acts as a stencil as it repels any colored slips, engobes, liquid underglazes or colored oxides thus leaving the white clay body exposed (Fig. 1-38A,B). *Always allow the wax to dry thoroughly before applying colors; otherwise any colors brushed over the pot and the wax will cause the colors to stick to the wax and destroy the design.*

All colored slips, engobes, liquid underglaze colors, and oxide colors must be thinned with water before applying them over a wax resist design. Several thin coats can be applied, but a thick coat of color may cover the wax pattern and the design will be lost.

Lines can be cut through the wax; the wax curl caused by cutting should then be brushed off and the lines filled in with contrasting color to create inlay patterns.

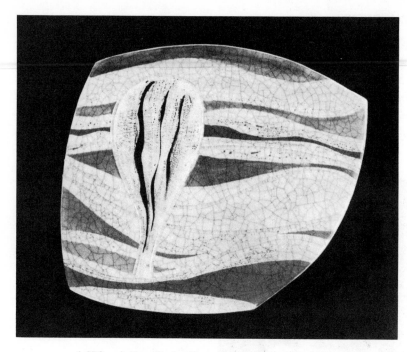

1-37A. Author. *Spring Tree*. Flat porcelain slab. Underglaze decoration on greenware. Wax resist over underglaze. Crackle glaze overall. Electric firing C/6. Diameter 10″.

1-37B. Close-up of 1-27A.

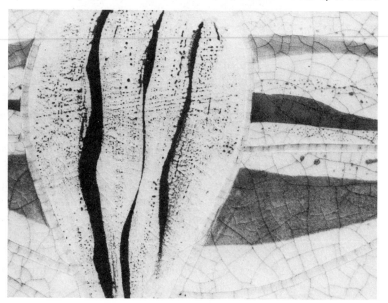

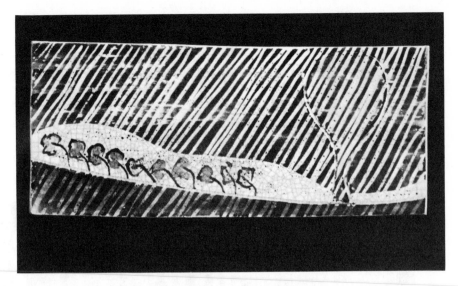

1-38A. Author. *Spring Rain*. Flat porcelain slab. Greenware waxed. Underglaze brushed overall. Crackle glaze poured over surface. Electric firing C/6. Diameter 10″.

1-38B. Close-up of 1-38A.

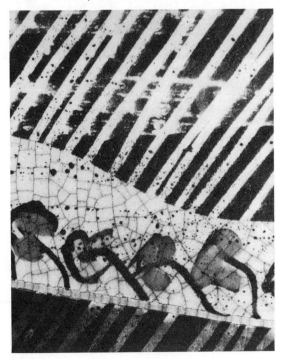

29

Multicolored decoration can be achieved by covering the wax resist design with a colored slip or engobe (Fig. 1-39A,B). Sections of the colored slip or engobe are reserved by painting some areas with wax before applying a different-colored slip or engobe.

When oxide colors are used over a wax resist pattern, water should be added to thin the oxide powder and a little feldspar, borax, or low-fire frit should be added to flux and harden the oxide on the pot after it is bisque-fired.

With the above uses of wax resist and colored slips, engobes,

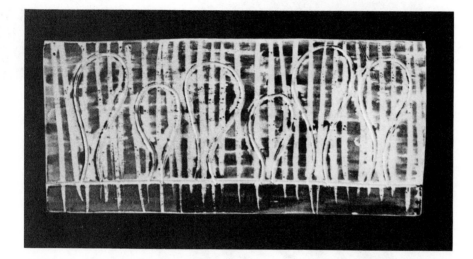

1-39A. Author. *Winter Trees.* Flat porcelain slab. Outline of trees cut into porcelain. Vertical lines waxed. Quick brushing with black underglaze over wax. Crackle glaze poured overall. Electric firing C/6. Diameter 10″.

1-39B. Close-up of 1-39A.

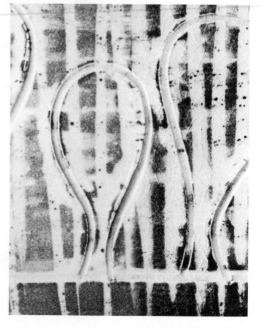

liquid underglazes and oxide colors, *it is best to do all decorating on damp, leather-hard greenware.* The dampness in the clay allows a thin coat of color to be applied more evenly over the body of the pot and across the wax resist pattern. The damp ware also allows the application of color to dry more slowly, thus ensuring adherence of the colors to the surface of the pot.

After the pot has been bisque-fired, a transparent glaze applied over the pot will allow the color to come through the glaze with a good color contrast design.

DECORATING CLAY IN THE DRY STATE

Once the clay form has dried, surface decoration is limited. *Moist clay cannot be added because the uneven drying of moist clay on a dry surface will cause the added clay to fall off during drying. The dry clay body cannot be moistened to permit adding clay. Forcing moisture into a dry clay form will cause the body to crack.*

1. ENGOBE DECORATION

This can be used on a dry pot (Fig. 1-40). Formulation of an engobe slip for dry ware allows this type of slip to dry quickly on the surface of the pot without moisture penetrating into the dry clay

1-40. Author. Wheel-thrown red stoneware vase. White engobe brushed on dry greenware. Blue engobe poured over white engobe. Transparent glaze overall. Gas reduction firing C/9. Height 14".

surface. The engobes can be sprayed or brushed on the dry clay surface. Allow each thin coat to dry slightly before adding another layer of engobe. Using a series of thinly sprayed coats works more successfully than trying to apply a single thick coat, which usually results in the engobe running unevenly over the surface. *Though engobes are in the clay slip family, the change in composition of the engobe allows use of this kind of slip on dry ware. A natural clay slip will not adhere to the dry body, as moisture from this slip is pulled into the dry clay body too quickly, which makes the slip flake off from the dry body.*

Cutting a pattern into the engobe surface is not advisable, as the engobe surface is hard and brittle. Cutting will cause the engobe to flake off from the dry clay surface.

2. UNDERGLAZE COLORS

These are concentrated ceramic oxide pigments which have been finely ground, calcined, and carefully washed. They are then compounded with special fluxes and modifiers for ease of application and color control (Fig. 1-41).

Commercial underglaze colors can be purchased in liquid form as semimoist cakes, and in pencil and crayon form. Opaque underglazes in 2-oz jars (Fig. 1-42) and transparent underglazes in ½-oz jars (Fig. 1-43) have the greatest range of colors. Semimoist cakes of color come 8 to a tin as transparent colors.

1-41. Author.
Spring-scape Bottle.
Wheel-thrown porcelain.
Underglaze decoration
brushed on greenware,
fired. Dipped in crackle
glaze, partially inked.
Electric firing C/6. Height 9″.

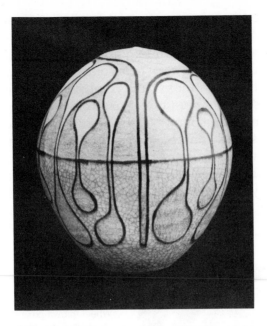

1-42. Author. *Reflections*. Wheel-thrown porcelain vase. Same process as 1-41. Electric firing C/6. Height 8″.

1-43. Author. *Spring Winds*. Porcelain slab construction. Underglaze decoration on greenware, bisque-fired. Crackle glaze poured over form, partially inked. Electric firing C/6. Height 16″.

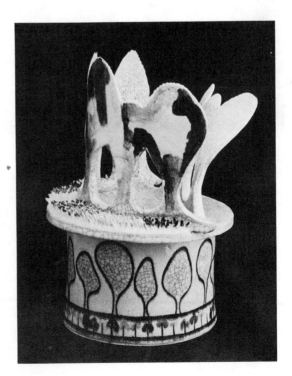

More limited in color range are the pencil and crayon forms of underglazes. They are opaque colors (Fig. 1-44A,B).

When ordering liquid underglaze colors, be sure to check a commercial color chart for specific colors. Most liquid underglaze colors have 3 to 6 variations of any color. The charts are available at any ceramic store selling underglaze colors.

Opaque and transparent liquid underglaze colors are best brushed on a slightly damp, leather-hard pot if large areas are to be covered. The moisture in the pot allows for a smooth brush surface (Fig. 1-45). One or several coats can be applied, each coat being allowed to dry before further application. For small areas or linear patterns, dry greenware can be painted with underglaze (Fig. 1-46).

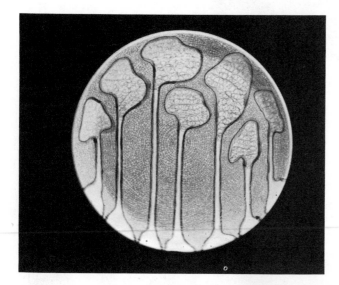

1-44A. Author. *Tree-scape.* Wheel-thrown porcelain plate. Green underglaze pencil and black liquid underglaze outline. Crackle glaze partially inked and wiped off after firing. Electric firing C/6. Diameter 16″.

1-44B. Close-up of 1-44A.

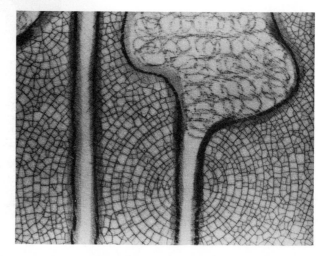

1-45. Author. *Tree-scape*.
Wheel-thrown porcelain plate. Black
underglaze line. Bisqued. Crackle
glaze partially inked and wiped off
after firing to bring out crackle. Electric
firing C/6. Diameter 16″.

1-46. Author. *Summer-scape*.
Wheel-thrown porcelain bottle.
Underglazes brushed on greenware,
fired. Crackle glaze partially inked to
bring out crackle after firing. Electric
firing C/6. Height 10″.

For best results the clay body should be white, or a dark-color
clay pot should first be covered with a white slip. The white
background is necessary to show the brilliance of color that underglazes can produce. If the underglaze colors are applied to a dark
body, the low contrast of clay and underglaze produces a loss of
color.

As a general rule, the pots are then bisque-fired to C/06 (1830°F) to harden the underglaze for glazing. *Do not use any colored glazes over the underglazes, as the total effect of the underglaze colors will be lost.* Generally a transparent, white gloss, or white mat glaze is used. The more transparent the glaze, the more brilliant the underglazes (Fig. 1-47). A white mat glaze will allow less of the color to come through and the color contrast will be softer. *Make tests with different base white glazes over the underglazes to see exacxtly what effect the glaze gives; then you can choose the best results* (Fig. 1-48).

Underglaze colors in a broad range of hue are limited as to the highest temperature at which they can be fired before some of the colors burn out (Fig. 1-49). *A safe firing range for all the colors is from a low of C/06 (1830°F) to a high of C/6 (2232°F).*

Generally, underglaze colors are fired in an electric kiln, though good results can be had by firing in a gas kiln as well. *The yellows, reds, and pinks will usually burn out if fired above C/6 (2232°F). The brown, blue, green and black underglazes will hold their color at the higher temperatures with a glaze over them.*

1-47. Author. Low bowl. Wheel-thrown porcelain. Underglaze wash on greenware, fired. Transparent glaze overall. Electric firing C/6. Diameter 8″.

1-48. Author. Covered jar. Wheel-thrown porcelain. Underglaze, fired. Vertical trees glazed with brush, then waxed over glaze and dipped into crackle glaze. Electric firing C/8. Height 8″.

1-49. Author. Wheel-thrown porcelain bottle. Underglaze applied on greenware. A thin turquoise wash with heavier color over wash, fired, glazed. Electric firing C/6. Height 6″.

Underglaze colors can also be fired to C/6 (2232°F) without a glaze over them. The surface remains dull but the colors are brilliant and durable (Fig. 1-50). With the unglazed method it is best to fire the underglaze around C/5 (2185°F) or C/6 (2232°F) to harden the underglaze on the pot. If fired at low temperatures, the underglaze might chip off.

1-50. Author. *Soul Food*. Porcelain slabs cut to resemble crackers, cheeses. Underglaze on all pieces. Some not glazed, leaving dull surface; others have a white mat glaze. Electric firing C/8. Diameter 16″.

Another variation of the use of underglaze without using a glaze over the colors contradicts the above statement that the underglaze retains a dull surface. I discovered accidentally that if the dry greenware is given a thin spray of underglaze and the pot fired to C/8 (2305°F) in an electric kiln, the underglaze fluxes slightly, which gives a soft sheen surface instead of a dull surface (Fig. 1-51). Even yellows retain their color in this process. This effect was observed when the underglaze was sprayed over porcelain greenware, and fired directly to C/8. However, this may not happen on all clays, so try a test first.

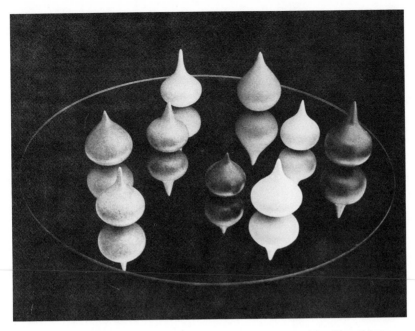

1-51. Author. *Reflections*. Wheel-thrown porcelain. Closed forms placed on mirrored glass for reflection. Underglaze sprayed thinly on unglazed greenware. Electric firing to C/8. Underglazes fluxed and produced a soft sheen. Bottle forms 3″ to 4″ high. Mirror diameter 18″.

1-52. Adam Sherman. Wheel-thrown red stoneware covered jar, reshaped and clay added. Gas reduction firing C/9. Height 14″.

2

Decorating Techniques on Bisqueware

Patricia McPheron. *Shadow Piece.* Low-fire clay structure with nylon fiber imbedded in clay for strength. Small plate form slip cast. Pieces bisque fired, then slowly smothered in a sawdust firing to create black surface. Cast shadow important to total structure. No glaze. Height 12″, width and depth 14″.

UNDERGLAZE PENCILS

Underglaze colors in pencil or crayon form seem to work better after the pot has been bisque-fired (Fig. 2-1A,B). Since the pot surface is hard, it is easier to use pressure on the bisque surface and produce a stronger line quality. Greenware does not accept color from an underglaze pencil as easily, and there is a tendency to dig into the softer greenware surface in order to get the linear design to accept the color. *Since the pencil or crayon design will be slightly powdery on the bisque pot surface, gently blow off any residue caused by the drawing and bisque-fire the pot again to C/06 (1830°F) to harden the design and make it easier to glaze.*

USE OF ENGOBES

Engobes can be formulated for application on bisqueware, glaze being then applied directly over the raw engobe (Fig. 2-2). Check the chart for engobes on bisqueware. For color, add oxides to the

41

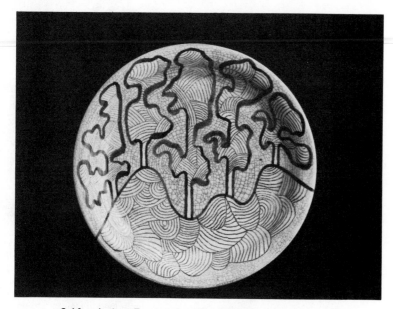

2-1A. Author. *Tree-scape*. Wheel-thrown porcelain platter. Underglaze decoration on greenware. Black underglaze outline applied with brush. Line pattern applied with green underglaze pencil after bisque firing. Crackle glaze overall. Electric firing C/6. Diameter 12″.

2-1B. Close-up of 2-1A.

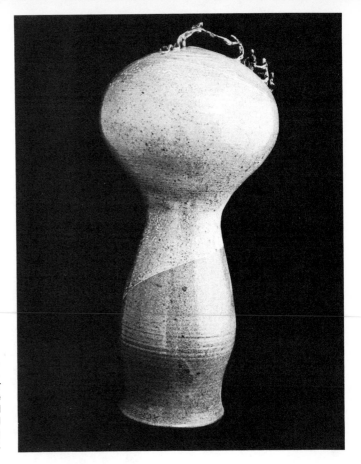

2-2. Author. *Top of the World.* Wheel-thrown stoneware in two sections. Figures applied. After bisque firing, lower section was masked and white bisque engobe was sprayed on. Figures were glazed with a brush while rest of form was sprayed with a transparent glaze. Gas reduction firing C/9. Height 30″.

dry powder, mix well, and add water. *Engobes for bisqueware should not be applied thickly, so a thin consistency is necessary.* Since the pot has already been bisque-fired, *the applied engobe must dry quickly with minimum shrinkage. This is the basic difference between a clay slip, which would dry and shrink off the bisqueware, and an engobe, which has minimum shrinkage and will adhere to the surface.*

USE OF OXIDES

With a raised or relief decoration, after the pot has been bisque-fired the surface can be sponged with a wet stain or iron oxide and water, which produces a clay color contrast of stained and unstained areas. This will yield a color contrast without glazing the surface. Unglazed surfaces stained with iron oxide will give a soft, dark sheen against the lighter unstained clay surfaces when the ware is fired between C/6 and C/9.

43

2-3. Eleanor Bravo. *Construction #2.* Stoneware clay reinforced with nylon fiber to prevent warping and shrinkage. Built with twisted clay coils, about ⅜″ diameter. Very slow drying. After bisque firing, red iron oxide sprayed over surface. No glaze. Fired at C/6. Height 32″, width 8″.

Earl McCutchen. Porcelain bowl. Transparent glaze
with wax resist and oxide wash over wax. Fired at C/9.
Diameter 7¾".

3

Testing Glazes and Colors

MAKING BASIC GLAZE TESTS

Glazes may be transparent or opaque and glossy or mat. They may
be low-fire C/010 Raku glazes or high-temperature glazes in the C/9
(2381°F) to C/12 (2419°F) range. The choice of glazes depends on the
temperature at which your clay body matures. There are glazes for
firing in electric kilns and glazes for firing in gas kilns. The variety
and colors of glazes are endless.

The only way to know if a glaze works on a clay body is to run a
test firing. *Never assume that because a glaze works on one clay body it
will also work on your clay body.* Ceramic books have a list of glaze
formulas to be fired at various temperatures. (Check the bibliography in the back of this book.) Choose glaze formulas in the firing
range in which you are working and include transparent, opaque
and glossy, and mat glazes in the tests. Also, try to choose glaze
formulas with the fewest glaze materials for your tests. If you do
this, you will not have to buy too many raw materials.

Bisque-fired test tiles have a horizontal and a vertical surface

TABLE 3.1   APPROXIMATE PERCENTAGES OF OXIDES TO USE IN A GLAZE

Oxide	Percentage	Oxidation	Reduction
Cobalt oxide	½	Medium blue	Medium blue
Cobalt oxide	2	Dark blue	Dark blue
Cobalt carbonate	½	Medium blue	Medium blue
Cobalt carbonate	2	Dark blue	Dark blue
Black copper oxide	½	Light green	Copper red–light green
Black copper oxide	2	Strong green	Copper red–strong green
Copper carbonate	2	Light green	Copper red–light green
Copper carbonate	5	Green	Copper red–dark green
Red iron oxide	2	Tan	Tan or gray-green
Red iron oxide	5	Brown	Brown or green
Red iron oxide	10	Dark brown	Reddish brown
Manganese dioxide	2	Tan	Tan
Manganese dioxide	5	Brown	Brown
Rutile, powdered	3	Tan	Tan
Rutile, powdered	8	Brown	Brown
Rutile, granular	5	Speckle brown	Speckle brown
Chromium oxide	2	Green	Green
Granular Illmanite	2	Black specks	Black specks
Cobalt carbonate ⎤	1		
Red iron oxide ⎦	2	Gray-blue	Gray-blue
Cobalt carbonate ⎤	½		
Copper carbonate ⎦	1	Blue-green	Blue-green
Cobalt oxide ⎤	1		
Red iron oxide	5		
Copper oxide ⎬	1	Black	Black
Manganese dioxide ⎦	5		

4. Weigh out at least 1,200 grams of dry base glaze. Although only 1,100 grams of base glaze is needed, it is better to have more so you don't run short.

5. Screen total amount of dry base glaze 2 or 3 times through a coarse sieve about window-screen mesh. Thorough mixing of the total dry glaze batch is very important, as this total batch is going to be divided.

6. Use 11 plastic sandwich bags. Weigh out 100 grams of the dry base glaze for each bag. Label each bag with the same number system as the 50-50 blend chart.

7. In each numbered bag with 100 grams of base glaze, add the corresponding percent of oxides. To find the amount of oxide needed in the 100 grams of glaze, the percentage is always multiplied by the total dry glaze batch. (*Example:* 100 grams glaze × 5% red iron oxide = 5 grams red iron oxide added in test #1.)

48

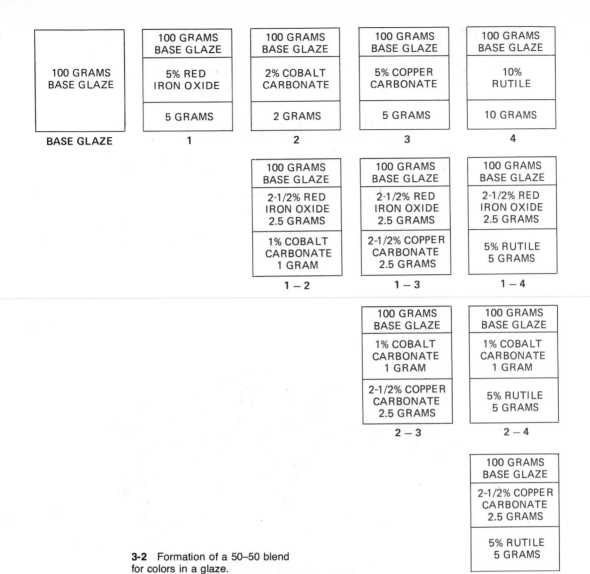

100 GRAMS BASE GLAZE	100 GRAMS BASE GLAZE	100 GRAMS BASE GLAZE	100 GRAMS BASE GLAZE	100 GRAMS BASE GLAZE
	5% RED IRON OXIDE	2% COBALT CARBONATE	5% COPPER CARBONATE	10% RUTILE
	5 GRAMS	2 GRAMS	5 GRAMS	10 GRAMS
BASE GLAZE	1	2	3	4

	100 GRAMS BASE GLAZE	100 GRAMS BASE GLAZE	100 GRAMS BASE GLAZE
	2-1/2% RED IRON OXIDE 2.5 GRAMS	2-1/2% RED IRON OXIDE 2.5 GRAMS	2-1/2% RED IRON OXIDE 2.5 GRAMS
	1% COBALT CARBONATE 1 GRAM	2-1/2% COPPER CARBONATE 2.5 GRAMS	5% RUTILE 5 GRAMS
	1 — 2	1 — 3	1 — 4

100 GRAMS BASE GLAZE	100 GRAMS BASE GLAZE
1% COBALT CARBONATE 1 GRAM	1% COBALT CARBONATE 1 GRAM
2-1/2% COPPER CARBONATE 2.5 GRAMS	5% RUTILE 5 GRAMS
2 — 3	2 — 4

100 GRAMS BASE GLAZE
2-1/2% COPPER CARBONATE 2.5 GRAMS
5% RUTILE 5 GRAMS
3 — 4

3-2 Formation of a 50–50 blend for colors in a glaze.

8. Take each bag with base glaze and oxides; put a small amount of water in a container, and then pour the dry glaze into the water. *Let the dry glaze disperse evenly through the water to prevent lumps.* Mix thoroughly to a creamy consistency; screen through a 30-mesh screen; and apply a thin and thick coat to the numbered test tile. Repeat this process for each bag of glaze and then fire the test tiles to the appropriate temperature.

9. *Do not try to predetermine what colors will result from these glaze tests. Every glaze will have a different effect on the coloring oxides in the glaze. Only by firing the glaze tests can you determine what colors will work for you.*

USE OF GLAZES

Glazes are basically glass coatings formulated to melt and adhere to the clay surface at various temperatures.

1. Do not use low-fire glazes on pots fired at high temperatures, as the glaze will run off the surface and over the kiln shelves.
2. Do not use high-temperature glazes in low-fire ranges, as the glaze will not mature, and this will result in a rough, underfired surface.
3. Generally, apply glazes to ware that has been bisque-fired and not to greenware. Greenware glazing requires special handling, longer drying periods between glaze coats, and glazes especially designed for application to greenware. If the greenware absorbs too much water from the glaze, the clay body may crack.

3-3. Barbara Schwartz. Porcelain plate. Hump mold shape, transparent glaze, black and silver lusters. Luster firing after transparent glaze fired first. Electric firing at C/018.

Author. Wheel-thrown, red stoneware
sculptural form. Shapes stacked.
White mat glaze overall. Wax-resist
pattern on raw glaze. Iron oxide
brushed overall to create pattern. Gas
reduction firing C/9. Height 30".

4

Decorative Techniques of Glaze Application

GLAZE APPLICATION

Similar methods of glaze application can be used regardless of the temperature to which the pot is fired. Results will vary when the same glaze is used over differently colored clay bodies and when the pot is fired in a reduction atmosphere in a gas kiln as opposed to an oxidizing atmosphere in an electric kiln.

Glaze consistency can vary according to whether the glaze is transparent, glossy, or mat.

Generally, a transparent glaze should be applied in a thin coating so that any decoration under the glaze comes through clearly. A transparent glaze will reflect the same color as the clay body beneath, giving a very bright, shiny surface.

Glossy and mat glazes can be applied in a heavier coat. Glossy glazes have a smooth, shiny surface, while mat glazes have a more dull, nonreflective surface. In an electric kiln firing, these glazes usually do not allow the clay body to show through the glaze; thus, differently colored clays will not greatly affect the glaze. In high-temperature reduction firing in a gas kiln, clay bodies will react through opaque-glossy and mat glazes, especially in red clay bodies if iron oxide is present. During reduction firing in a gas kiln at C/9 (2336°F) to C/10 (2381°F), all glazes interact with the iron or impurities in the clay bodies. Some mat glazes fired at C/9 to C/10 in a gas reduction atmosphere show a radical difference in color in thin and in thick application. Glazes using spodumene and Cornwall stone have this characteristic.

POURING AND DIPPING GLAZES

When pouring or dipping glazes on a pot, you must be sure to have a good quantity of glaze (Figs. 4-1 through 4-3). Make at least 600 grams of glaze. *This will fill a quart jar including water. Around 2,000 grams of glaze with water will fill a 1-gallon jar. About 7,500 to 10,000 grams of glaze with water will fill a 5-gallon pail.* Allow the glaze to soak thoroughly into the water; stir and screen several times through a 30-mesh screen.

4-1. Author. Wheel-thrown red stoneware bottles. Glaze pattern poured on bottles. Then glazed areas waxed and bottles dipped into contrasting glaze. Gas reduction firing C/9. Height 6″.

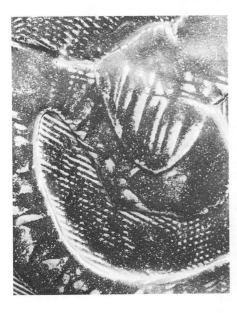

4-2A. Author. Large red stoneware slab platter with added slabs of clay and textured surfaces. Low relief. One glaze poured overall. Color break from glazes thinning out on edges of textured surfaces during firing. Gas reduction firing C/9. Diameter 16″.

4-2B. Close-up of 4-2A.

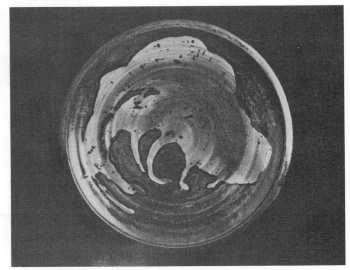

4-3. Author. Wheel-thrown red stoneware plate. One glaze poured in center, then waxed. Darker glaze poured overall for two-color pattern. Gas reduction firing C/9. Diameter 10″.

Always stir glazes before you use them. When glazes are not used, even for a short time, the glaze materials settle to the bottom, leaving water on top. This water must always be thoroughly mixed with the glaze before using. It is best to wax the foot of the pot and up the side about ¼ inch to ½ inch before glazing.

After glazing, wipe off any glaze adhering to the wax to keep the pot from sticking to the shelf during firing.

If the ceramic form is a container shape, pour the glaze inside first. Then, let the pot dry thoroughly before dipping or pouring glaze on the outside of the shape. Overlapping will change or deepen the color (Figure 4-4).

When differently colored glazes are used, also allow the glazes to overlap. This overlap can produce an interesting third color. You cannot presume what the overlap of two colored glazes will produce until after the firing. Keep notes as to which glaze was over the other, because a reverse dip or pour can produce a different result. *In fact, keep careful notes of what you put on the pot, because results can be quite different from the mental image you had of the fired product.*

4-4. Author. Wheel-thrown red stoneware bottle vase. Form pushed in immediately after throwing. Vase dipped into glaze. Second application of same glaze poured over form created a double thickness and resulted in change of color from brown to tan where thick. Gas reduction firing C/9. Height 10″.

SPRAYING GLAZES

Sprayed glazes will give you a uniform coat of glaze as well as subtle variations of color (Fig. 4-5). There is a greater waste of glaze since much of the spray ends up in the spray booth. *Since many glazes are toxic, a well-ventilated spray booth is a necessity. Also, wearing of a face mask or respirator should always be a rule to keep from inhaling any of the glaze particles.*

The glaze used in a spray gun should be of a thinner consistency than that used for dipping or pouring. If a wet coat of glaze is sprayed on the pot, the glazed pot is easier to handle afterwards, because the raw glaze surface has a hard finish similar to that of dipped and poured glazes. This *wet spray* is achieved by holding the spray gun close to the pot. To prevent the glaze from running, continually turn the pot while spraying and do not overlap the wet sprayed areas. It is a little tricky, but practice will help you master the technique!

If the spray gun is held too far away from the pot, the glaze particles become air-dried before they hit the pot, and a pebbly surface results. This pebbly surface is very hard to handle without having the glaze come off on your hands, and the edges of the glaze easily chip off as well. If a vegetable glue such as sodium Carboxymethylcellulose (CMC) is added to the glaze, the result is a harder glaze that does not dust off the pot easily.

4-5. Joe Bova. *Funkplane*. Wheel-thrown white clay. Sections reshaped and put together. Thin spray of underglaze covered by transparent glaze. Mother-of-pearl luster overall. Electric firing C/4. Diameter 18″.

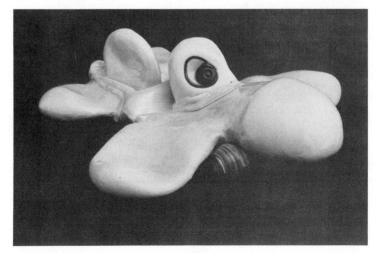

Do not spray glaze over a wax resist design. The fine spray will stick to the wax and diffuse the design.

Forms with delicate designs in or on the surface are well suited for spraying, especially if you only want a thin coat of glaze over the pot.

Be sure to clean the spray gun immediately after spraying. The interior mechanism easily clogs if the glaze dries in the gun. Use water for cleaning.

If a great deal of spraying is done, the spray booth walls will become coated with glazes of all types and colors that you have been using. Scrape the glaze off the walls, add water, soak, and screen the glaze. Fire a test tile to see what color the mixture becomes. Label this scrap glaze "Bastard Glaze" and use it on future pots. The term is appropriate since the glaze is a combination of unknown proportions of glazes and colors which, when used up, cannot be repeated.

Generally this scrap glaze can be very successfully used by itself on pots and in combination with other glazes. This process of salvaging old glazes and intermixing them can be done any time with any scraps fired at about the same temperatures.

BRUSHING GLAZES

Glazes that can be successfully brushed on a pot for total glazing include (1) commercially prepared liquid glazes and (2) transparent glazes which you make up from batch formulas. Commercially prepared glazes are usually in the low-fire range of C/06 (1830°F) to C/04 (1940°F). They are specially prepared glazes to be brushed on the surface of the pot. *Be sure to follow directions as to how many coats of glaze are needed.* Use a soft, flat-edge brush and crisscross applications for best results. Transparent glazes fired at various temperatures from C/06 (1830°F) to C/10 (2381°F) can be brushed on the pot. Brush marks will generally smooth out in firing because such glazes will melt evenly.

Any other glazes made up from basic glaze formulas work best if the pot is dipped in the glaze, the glaze is poured on the pot, or the glaze is sprayed on the total pot. If these glazes are brushed on the bisque pot, it is difficult to get an even coat of glaze; therefore, after firing, the thick-thin application results in a blotchy, uneven glaze surface unless a binder is used.

If it is necessary to brush glazes, other than commercially prepared glazes, on the pot, then a binder must be added in order to give a smooth coat on the surface of the pot. Gum arabic or tragacanth is usually used as a binder. The granular gum crystals, weighing about ¼ oz, are soaked in water overnight and the mixture is then stirred quickly to a creamy consistency to produce about a quart of binder. A couple of drops of carbolic acid are added to prevent decomposition of the mixture so that it can be used as needed. One or two teaspoons of this solution per quart of wet glaze will allow for adequate brushing of the glaze on the pot.

As a temporary binder, sugar syrup or wheat flour can be added to a portion of wet glaze for adherence to the pot.

All these binders work best when: (1) reglazing a pot after the glaze firing to get a thicker coat of glaze; (2) a bisque firing goes too high and the bisqueware is too dense to accept enough raw glaze; or (3) fritted glazes that contain little or no raw clay in the formula are used. The gum, syrup, or wheat flour burns out completely during the firing.

Brushing a glaze over another glaze in small areas, using fast single brush strokes, or even brushing small areas on the bisqueware will work well (Figs. 4-6 through 4-9). Do not use stiff oil-painting brushes, as they do not hold enough glaze. Large Japanese watercolor brushes and wide, soft, watercolor brushes are the best to use for any kind of surface decoration.

4-6. Author. *Bowl with Ground Squirrels*. Wheel-thrown red stoneware with forms added to rim. Animals glazed with brush and waxed. Second glaze poured over the bowl for color contrast. Gas reduction firing C/9. Diameter 14″.

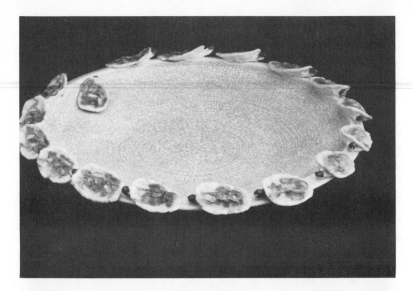

4-7. Author. *Turtle Bowl.*
Wheel-thrown porcelain with
added turtle forms. Turtles glazed
with brush, iron oxide applied over
glaze, then forms waxed. Crackle
glaze poured overall and inked to
bring out crackle after firing.
Electric firing C/8. Diameter 16″.

4-8. Author. *Bear Bowl.*
Wheel-thrown red stoneware.
Process same as 4-7. Light tan
glaze poured overall and dark
brown glaze poured over tan for
color break. Gas reduction firing
C/9. Diameter 14″.

4-9. Author. *Bread Board.*
Porcelain slab slices cut, dried,
and fired together. Glaze brushed
on edges. Electric firing C/8.
Diameter 18″.

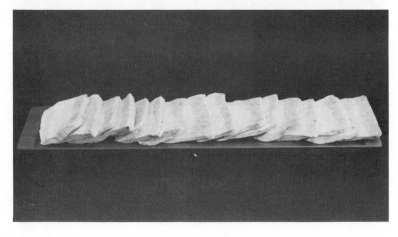

COLORED OXIDES FOR DECORATION

Coloring oxides are obtained in powder form. They are the same metallic oxides you add to a base glaze for color. They can be used by themselves for decorative brushwork over a glaze. Water is added to the oxides and then brushed over the already applied, unfired glaze and fired.

As a general rule, do not brush the oxides on the bisqueware under the glaze. When the oxides dry on the unglazed bisqueware, they leave a powdery surface. If the oxide has been applied a little too thickly, then applying the glaze over the oxide is like applying the glaze over a layer of dust on the surface of the pot. *The glaze, when fired, will crawl away from the oxide surface, leaving bare spots on the clay form because the glaze does not adhere to the powdered oxide surface.*

Basic Coloring Oxides for Use Over a Glaze

1. Red iron oxide (brown)
2. Black iron oxide (brown)
3. Rutile (tan)
4. Copper oxide black (green)
5. Copper carbonate (green)
6. Cobalt oxide (blue)
7. Cobalt carbonate (blue)
8. Yellow ochre (tan)
9. Manganese dioxide (brown)
10. Burnt umber (brown)

The oxides can be applied over any glaze at any firing range from C/06 through C/12 (1830°F through 2419°F), fired in electric or gas reduction kilns (Fig. 4-10).

Transparent and glossy glazes under the oxides may cause the oxide decoration to run or feather a little because the glazes do flow slightly during firing, but the effect is pleasing and uniform.

Mat glazes generally do not move in firing. The dense glaze surface will hold the oxide decoration where you put it because the glaze fluxes less than transparent or gloss glazes (Figs. 4-11 and 4-12). *It is a good rule not to cover the total glaze surface with any oxide, as some oxides have a slight fluxing quality and might make the glaze flow in firing, causing the glaze to run off the pot and stick to the shelf.* To play safe, do not apply extensive oxides to the lower quarter of the pot in order to allow for any additional pulling of the glaze and oxide

4-10. Author. Sculpture form. Wheel-thrown red stoneware shapes stacked. White glaze poured over shapes. Cobalt and iron oxides brushed over glaze. Gas reduction firing C/9. Height 30″.

4-11. Author. Wheel-thrown red stoneware vase. Dipped in tan mat glaze. Cobalt and iron oxide brushed over glaze. Gas reduction firing C/9. Height 10″.

4-12. Maurice Grossman. *Love Pot and Warrior.* A slab-built pot with stiff, blue mat glaze. Iron oxide brushed on warrior. Unglazed. Both gas reduction firing C/9. Height 5″.

towards the base of the pot during firing. Once you have tested certain glazes and oxides and you know the oxide will remain stationary, then there is no problem!

Generally, white or light-colored glazes give the best base for an overlay of any of the oxides (Fig. 4-13). The lighter or whiter the glaze, the greater the contrast in color. *Do not assume that any one oxide color will be the same over one glaze as over another glaze. Different glazes and firing temperatures will vary the color of the oxide.* Red or black iron oxide may vary from yellow-tan to brown; rutile will break in color from tan to soft yellow to blue; copper can give any number of variations of green; cobalt can go from blue to purple; manganese dioxide can give brown to purple. *Another variation in the color of any oxide depends on whether it is fired in an oxidizing atmosphere in an electric kiln or in the reducing atmosphere of a gas kiln.*

If the oxides are mixed to a thin consistency (with too much water), the color will not be strong; if the oxides are mixed with too little water, they may flux the glaze and run or blister. *Cobalt oxide and copper oxide will turn black over a glaze if the water and oxide combination is too thick.* Cobalt oxide and copper oxide are very strong colors, and a more watery consistency will give a strong blue or green. Cobalt carbonate *is easier to disperse in water than cobalt*

61

4-13. Author. Red stoneware, slab-built compote. Thick white porcelain clay added with finger impressions. Colored slip added to top porcelain impressions. Iron oxide added to lower porcelain clay forms. Translucent glaze overall. Gas reduction firing C/9. Height 10".

oxide and it gives just as strong a blue. If you want to soften the strong intensity of the cobalt blue color, add a little red iron oxide to the watery mixture.

BRUSHING OXIDE DECORATION

Brushing oxides over a glaze to create a design takes a little practice (Fig. 4-14). First, the brush should be a soft-hair brush which will hold a lot of wet oxide. Japanese watercolor brushes are ideal for this because the tip of the brush comes to a fine point while the body of the brush can produce a heavy stroke of color. For broad areas of oxide decoration, use a flat-edge watercolor brush.

To determine where you want to place a pattern, draw lightly over the raw glaze surface with a pencil, indicating where you want the brush design. Use the pencil pattern only as a general indication of the design. This is not a fill-in-between-the-line approach. The pencil marks will burn out during firing. Hold the brush loosely near the end. Do not hold the brush as tightly as you would a pencil or pen. All brush movement comes from the wrist, with little or no movement of the arm.

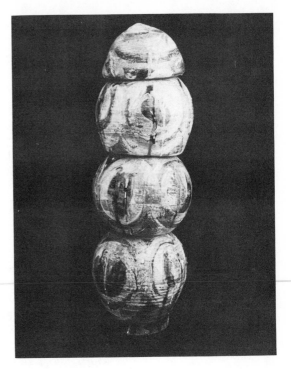

4-14. Author. *Totem*. Wheel-thrown red stoneware forms stacked. White and blue slip applied on greenware. Copper, rutile, and iron oxides applied over transparent glaze. Gas reduction firing C/9. Height 30″.

Practice on a piece of large paper with continuous movement, using the top of the brush to create fine lines. Then bear down on the brush for a strong, heavy stroke (Fig. 4-15). India ink works

4-15. Author. Large, wheel-thrown, white stoneware platter. Crackle glaze poured on surface. Iron and cobalt oxides brushed over glaze. After firing, glaze inked to bring out crackle. Electric firing C/8. Diameter 18″.

well for this practice. Since we are not "born" with a brush as a writing tool, as are the Japanese and Chinese, it will take practice to discover the elegance of a brush stroke with its many variations.

WAX RESIST DECORATION

This form of decoration on the bisque pot has many variations, in combination with glazes, oxides, and the use of the unglazed clay surface.

1. Glaze the total pot with a white or light-colored glaze and allow the glaze to dry (Fig. 4-16). With the brush, apply a wax design over the raw, unfired glaze. After the wax dries, brush an oxide around the wax pattern; or pour or dip the pot into a darker, contrasting glaze as a second layer. *Be sure the second glaze is thin or it will cover the wax pattern.* Where the glaze is waxed, the original white glaze will show up in contrast to the darker oxide pattern or darker applied glaze (Figs. 4-17A,B; 4-18). *If small particles of glaze or oxide stick to the wax, it is not necessary to wipe them off. The particles create an interesting mottled effect on the base glaze.*

2. Brush an oxide design directly on the raw, dry glaze surface of the pot. Wax the oxide and part of the base glaze around the oxide. Allow the wax to dry. Then take another colored oxide and brush around the wax areas. This creates a three-color design.

4-16. Author. Wheel-thrown red stoneware bottle. White mat glaze overall. Wavy lines waxed, then cobalt and iron oxides brushed over total surface, leaving white glaze where waxed. Gas reduction firing C/9. Height 7".

4-17A. Author. Wheel-thrown, white stoneware, low bowl. White mat glaze overall. Iron oxide decoration applied directly over white glaze. Oxide and part of white glaze waxed to create a halo effect. Cobalt oxide with a little iron oxide brushed overall. Electric firing C/8. Diameter 16″.

4-17B. Close-up of 4-17A.

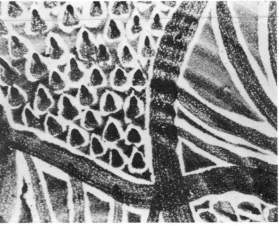

4-18. Author. Wheel-thrown, red stoneware sculpture form. Bisque form waxed. White mat glaze poured overall, leaving waxed areas unglazed. Gas reduction firing C/9. Height 24″.

3. Wax a design directly on the unglazed bisque pot (Figs. 4-19, 4-20). If a dark clay body is used, then pour or dip a white or light-colored glaze over the pot. If the clay is white, pour or dip a dark-colored glaze over the form. Either approach exposes the unglazed fired clay contrasting with the glazed areas.

4-19. Author. Wheel-thrown white stoneware vase. Background of the bisqued pot waxed, leaving the figure in glazed relief when the vase dipped into stiff mat glaze. Gas reduction firing C/9. Height 12″.

4-20. Author. Wheel-thrown porcelain shallow bowls. White mat glaze overall. Iron oxide brushed directly over raw glaze and waxed line. Electric firing C/8. Diameter 7″.

SGRAFFITO AND MISHIMA INLAY

These techniques usually work best over a light-colored mat glaze that will not run or move on the pot during the firing; otherwise the linear pattern will be lost. The term *sgraffito* means cutting into a surface to create a line design. *Mishima* is a Korean term for the method of getting color into a line. These methods are also mentioned in the section on greenware.

The pot is glazed with a white or light-colored mat glaze and allowed to dry (Fig. 4-21). An area of the dry glaze is waxed and thoroughly dried. About 30 minutes should be allowed for drying. At this time, a sharp-pointed tool is used to cut a linear pattern through the wax to the glaze. Then with a soft, dry brush, the curled edges of the wax are gently brushed off, leaving a clean line (Fig. 4-22). A small pointed brush is used with oxide or a dark glaze to fill in the line. The oxide will not adhere to the wax, so the line design can be filled quickly (Fig. 4-23). The wax will burn out during the firing. *If you are firing an electric kiln and have many pots with wax designs, leave the kiln door open 2 or 3 inches for 1 hour to burn off the wax and allow the wax residue to get out of the kiln. This keeps your kiln clean and prevents any wax residue from coating the heating elements.*

4-21. Author. Wheel-thrown porcelain bowl. Sgraffito decoration cut through waxed surface to mat glaze. Iron oxide painted into line. Electric firing C/8. Height 8″.

4-22. Author. Wheel-thrown porcelain bottle. Same decoration as 4-21. Electric firing C/8. Height 6″.

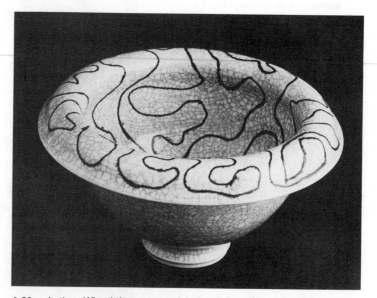

4-23. Author. Wheel-thrown porcelain bowl. Sgraffito and mishima techniques same as 4-21 and 4-22. Electric firing C/8. Height 7″.

4-24. Cloyde Snook. Wheel-thrown, stoneware, covered jar. Iron and cobalt oxides brushed lightly over glaze. Gas reduction firing C/10. Height 18″.

Caryn Ostrowe. *The Exercist Doll Doing Pushups.*
Porcelain face with underglazes, maribou feathers,
fabric, and stuffing. Height 14″.

5

Glaze Defects

Most problems with glaze defects come from careless handling or application of the glaze; using the wrong glaze at the wrong temperature; or just being in too much of a hurry to get those pots into the kiln. Practice eliminates many problems if you can recognize what went wrong. There are times when glaze materials change in composition and your favorite mat glaze becomes glossy. This can drive any potter crazy!

Firing at a different altitude in a gas kiln may change the character of a glaze. But there are basic problems which need not happen.

BODY AND APPLICATION DEFECTS

Do not bisque-fire the greenware under C/06 (1830°F). The clay body will be too soft and porous. When the glaze is poured or the pot is dipped into the glaze, the extreme porosity will give a glaze thickness you do not want.

Pinholes on the raw glaze surface can occur for two reasons. First, the fresh bucket of glaze may have been stirred quickly, which results in the accumulation of air bubbles in the glaze. When the pot is dipped in the glaze, these air pockets cling to the pot surface. Stir the glaze gently to prevent air bubbles. Second, if the pot is dipped too quickly into the glaze, air pockets can form on the surface of the glaze. A second thin dip may eliminate the air pockets. If the pinholes persist, gently rubbing the dry glaze surface can seal them over. *If the pinholes are still left, they may not seal over after the firing. This is more true with stiff mat glazes.*

Dust on the surface of the bisque pot or grease from handling the pot with perspiring hands can prevent bond formation between the glaze and the body. This can result in the glaze "crawling," which leaves bare spots on the clay surface after firing. *Always blow any dust off the pot and wipe the pot with a damp sponge before glazing to eliminate these problems.*

If a colored glaze is too thin when applied, the color will be poor. With a thin mat glaze, the surface will be rough. *If you can see the texture of the bisque body through the glaze, the application is too thin. Apply another coat of glaze.*

Some glazes have a tendency to show hairline cracks after drying on the pot. Lightly rub the glaze surface to seal the cracks.

If the glaze is applied too heavily, wide cracks will appear which cannot be sealed. If the pot is fired, these cracks will widen and the glaze will pull away, leaving bare spots. The best thing to do is: (1) scrape the glaze off the pot and let it dry; (2) thin the glaze with water and reglaze.

When overlapping one glaze over the other, do not let the first glaze dry completely, or the second overlapped glaze may try to pull away from the first glaze. This is because the moisture is being drawn out of the overlapped glaze at too fast a rate. This does no harm on a horizontal surface, as the glaze will seal down during the firing. On a vertical surface, the raw glaze will flake off before you get it to the kiln. Scrape the glaze off the pot and start over again.

DEFECTS IN FIRING

Underfired pots have a rough, immature surface. *These pots can be refired to the correct temperature and the glaze will be mature.*

Overfiring may cause the glaze to run off the pot's surface and all over the shelves. What a mess! Most glazes have a 2- or 3-cone range, which lessens the problem of over- or underfiring.

73

Never put freshly glazed pots in the kiln and fire them immediately. The hot moisture will cause the glaze to blister and possibly crawl, leaving bare spots on the clay surface.

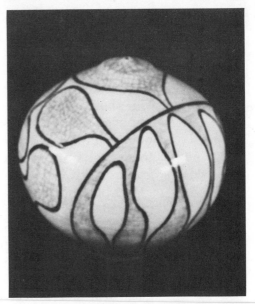

Author. Wheel-thrown porcelain vase. Linear pattern on greenware created with liquid underglaze, pencil underglaze in light areas, crackle glaze overall. India ink brushed in specific areas and wiped off. Electric firing C/6. Height 10″, width 7″.

6

Types of Glazes

LOW-FIRE COMMERCIAL GLAZES

These prepared liquid glazes generally come in 4-ounce jars and they are formulated to be used only for brushing on the bisque-ware. The glazes are fired in a range of C/06 (1830°F) to C/04 (1940°F). Because of this low temperature, there is a broad spectrum of colors available. Color charts, which illustrate all available colors, can be obtained from any ceramic supplier. As with the liquid underglazes, there are many variations of any one color available, so it is important to check the colors to see which yellow, blue, green, etc., you may want to use. A soft, flat-edge, 1-inch, watercolor brush is ideal for brushing large areas of the pot. The glazes come in transparent, opaque, glossy, and mat surfaces, and in addition many glazes give mottled effects. *Be very sure to follow the directions as to how many coats of glaze to apply. Always crisscross coats of glaze.* If these glazes are not applied heavily enough, the color will be lost. This is especially true of bright red and orange glazes.

These glazes work best when fired in an electric kiln in an oxidation atmosphere. Unlike high-fire glazes, these low-fire glazes can be applied down to the bottom edge of the pot. The bottom can also be glazed. Triangular clay stilts are placed on the kiln shelf and the pot is set on the stilts. After firing, the pot is removed and the stilts pulled off the glazed surface, leaving small points of unglazed surface which do not affect the appearance of the glazed bottom of the pot. *This process of using stilts is best for low-fire work.*

It is possible to fire a piece with high-temperature glazes to C/6 (2232°F) or C/9 (2336°f) leaving areas unglazed on the pot, and then come back and brush low-fire glazes on these unglazed areas and refire at low temperature. It will take more coats of glaze to do this, as the pot will be more vitrified, which causes each coat to be thinner as it is applied to a nonporous surface. Each coat of low-fire glaze will take longer to dry, but interesting results can be obtained.

LOW-FIRE RAKU GLAZES

Raku glazes can range from C/010 (1641°F) to C/06 (1830°F), and they can be used in a smoky reduction atmosphere or an oxidation atmosphere. The term *instant pots* relates to the fast firing of these pots in a time span of 20 to 30 minutes, whereas in other firing procedures the glazed ware is usually fired for 6 to 12 hours depending on temperature.

These glazes are usually simple in composition. Many of these Raku glazes contain borax, which is water-soluble. *After mixing the glaze with water, keep a tight cover on the glaze when it is not being used.* If the water evaporates, there is a loss of borax, and adding more water will weaken this flux, change the glaze composition, and possibly cause the glaze not to melt in firing.

There are many excellent books on the process of Raku firing. Refer to the bibliography in the back of this book.

LOW-FIRE EARTHENWARE GLAZES

Another range of low-fire glazes is from C/06 (1830°F) to C/2 (2124°F). In this range, especially for C/06 (1830°F) to about C/02 (2048°F), many glazes have traditionally used lead carbonate (white lead) or red lead as the major flux to get bright colors. *White*

6.1 Author. *Exercise Pot.* Wheel-thrown, red stoneware, added figures. Glaze poured overall. Gas reduction firing C/9. Height 14″, width 12″.

and red lead are very poisonous! Do not breathe any dust from the dry material. Use a paper face mask and wash your hands after handling dry lead. Lead is soluble after the glaze has been fired. Never store acids such as lime or lemon juice, tea, fruit juice, etc., in a bowl with a lead glaze. The acid in these juices will draw the lead out of the fired glaze and bring it into solution with the juice.

Lead glazes can be used on vases of any shape and any sculptural form. As substitutes for raw lead glazes, there are fritted glazes containing lead. *Frit* is commercially made by melting a lead glaze and grinding it to a fine mesh. The frit is added to the glaze formula as a major flux. This process renders the lead insoluble and free from any poisonous effects.

These frits are listed by number, such as Ferro 3396 or Pemco 24, with the name indicating the company of manufacture. Frits can be purchased from most ceramic supply stores. There are lead-containing and leadless frits. There also are borax frits such as Ferro 3134 or 3223. The borax is rendered insoluble when used in a fritted form.

HIGH-FIRE GLAZES

High-fire glazes range in firing temperature from C/6 (2232°F) to C-12 (2419°F). They can be used on stoneware or porcelain clays and can be fired in an electric kiln or a gas kiln. Usually glaze formulas indicate whether they are for electric or gas reduction firing. This does not limit using glazes for gas reduction firing in an electric kiln or vice versa. There will be a change in color and surface of the glaze in this transfer due to the change in the oxidation atmosphere in the electric kiln and reduction atmosphere in the gas kiln. This type of experimentation can prove interesting.

SPECIAL NOTES ON USES
OF SOME CHEMICALS IN GLAZES

1. BARIUM CARBONATE

When barium carbonate is used in a glaze, the total glaze batch should be screened wet through a 30-mesh screen at least 2 or 3 times. A rubber spatula should be used to work the wet glaze through the screen. This is done to break down the particles of the barium carbonate as well as to give a thorough mix to the glaze batch. *If the barium carbonate is not thoroughly broken down, small white specks will appear on the glaze surface. The barium specks will not melt down in firing and will thus remain as rough spots on the fired glaze.*

2. TIN OXIDE, OPAX, ZIRCOPAX, SUPERPAX, AND ULTROX

The above oxides are all opacifiers. Their main purpose in a glaze is to produce a white glaze base. Tin oxide is the best and strongest of the opacifiers; the others are synthetic and weaker in producing a white base glaze. Because tin oxide is 3 to 4 times more costly, the synthetic opacifiers can be substituted. For any glaze that calls for tin oxide, opax, zircopax, superpax, or ultrox can be used by doubling the amount of oxide called for in the glaze. The only exception, where a substitute for tin oxide cannot be used, is in copper-red glazes. Here the tin oxide is critical in helping to produce the copper-red glazes in gas reduction firing. A substitute for tin oxide will cause a loss of color and character of the copper-red glazes.

Plate 1
Author. Vase, wheel thrown with added figures unglazed.
Model-car gold enamel painted on figure after completed firing.
Gas reduction C/9. Height 12".

Plate 2 (right)
Maurice Grossman. *North Mountain Box.*
Stoneware clay, slab construction, wax-resist
decoration with semi-mat glaze. Gas fired.
Height 23″, width 16″.

Plate 3 (below)
Author. Three landscape covered jars with
figures. Wheel-thrown porcelain. Underglaze
decoration on greenware. Transparent crackle
glaze overall. Crackle glaze brushed with India
ink in areas and wiped off. Electric firing C/8.
Height, left to right: 12″, 10″, 9″.

Plate 4 (left)
Author. *Everblooms*. Wheel-thrown, two-piece, red-stoneware form. Added clay surfaces unglazed. After gas reduction C/9 firing, clay surfaces painted with model-car enamels. Height 30″.

Plate 5 (below)
Joe Bova. *Masta Gator*. White stoneware, bisque fired to C/6, China paints brushed on clay surface, no glaze, fired to C/016. Electric firing. Length 22″, height 7″, width 12″.

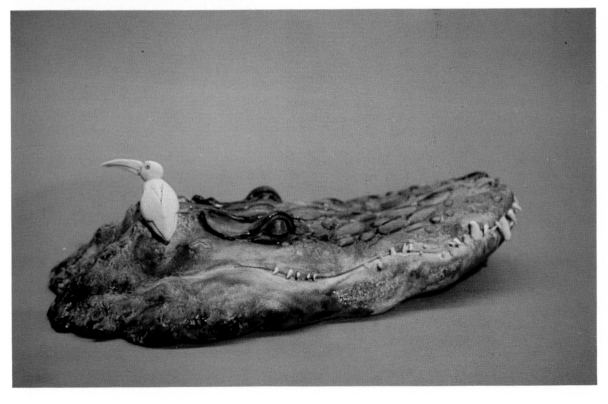

Plate 11 (above right)
Patti Warashina. *Trojan Car*. Low-fire clay, decorated with underglaze, glaze, luster glaze, plexiglass windows. C/06 and C/018. Electric firing. Length 36".

Plate 12 (middle right)
Rick Dillingham. Raku vase. Hand-built, bisque dried, purposely broken, refired. Gold-leaf design applied, then reassembled and grouted. Diameter 18".

Plate 13 (bottom right)
Patti Warashina. *Before the Catch*. Covered fish plate, low-fire clay, underglaze decoration with transparent glaze. Firing C/06, electric kiln. Length 24".

Plate 14
Author. Planter. Wheel-thrown, red-stoneware planter. Form
turned upside down. Thick, white-porcelain slip poured over pot.
Second pouring of blue-porcelain slip poured over white slip on
damp greenware. Glossy off-white glaze overall. Gas reduction
firing C/9. Height 14″, width 12″.

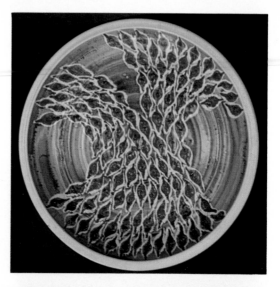

Plate 15 (below left)
Barbara Schwartz. *Porcelain Plate.* Hump-mold
shape, transparent glaze fired first, then
multicolors of lusters painted and fired again
to C/018. Electric firing.

Plate 16 (above right)
Author. Low bowl. Wheel-thrown, red-
stoneware clay, white-gloss glaze overall, wax-
resist pattern over raw glaze filled in with iron
oxide. Iron oxide waxed, mixture of cobalt carbonate and iron oxide brushed over total surface.
Gas reduction firing C/9. Diameter 18".

Plate 17 (middle right)
Author. Shallow bowl. Wheel-thrown white
stoneware. Liquid transparent underglaze
applied on greenware as a wash. Transparent
glaze overall. Electric firing C/8.

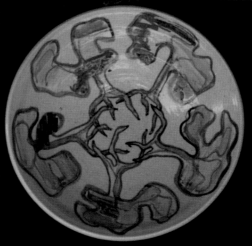

Plate 18 (bottom right)
Author. Large, low bowl. Slab-constructed red
stoneware in a plaster mold. Off-white glaze
overall. Cobalt, copper-iron oxide brushed
directly over glaze. Gas reduction firing C/6.
Diameter 24".

3. FELDSPAR SUBSTITUTION

Feldspars, which are a part of almost all glazes, are divided into two types, potash (potassium) and soda (sodium) feldspars. There are times when one of the feldspars you are using in a glaze becomes unavailable and a substitution must be made.

Potash feldspars such as Buckingham, Kingman, and Custer feldspar can be substituted for each other because their compositions are similar.

Soda feldspars, such as nepheline, syenite, and Kona-F4, can also be substituted for each other for the same reason. *Do not substitute soda feldspars for potash feldspars because the soda feldspars have a greater fluxing quality, and the overall character of the glaze will change.*

4. CALCINED KAOLIN

If calcined kaolin is called for in a glaze, you can purchase it or easily make your own. Calcined kaolin differs from regular kaolin in that the chemical water has already been driven out of the kaolin by heat, thus making it more refractory when used in a glaze. Simply take a bisque-fired bowl, fill it with kaolin as it comes out of the bag in powder form, and fire it to C/06. Then use it in the glaze formula as calcined kaolin.

5. GERSTLEY BORATE (COLEMANITE)

The names Gerstley borate and colemanite will be used interchangeably in glaze formulas to denote a strong fluxing agent in glazes at all temperatures. When ordering this chemical, always ask for *Gerstley borate* by name. If you ask for colemanite, you might get a synthetically produced product, which could ruin your glazes.

6. BENTONITE

Bentonite is a very fine, extremely plastic clay of volcanic origin. There are some glazes which will settle to the bottom of the container in a hard mass when mixed with water, making it difficult to stir them into solution before using the glaze. Bentonite is added to the glaze to keep it in suspension in the water and prevent hard settling. *When weighing out the dry materials for a glaze, add the bentonite to the dry mixture and mix it well with the other dry chemicals before adding water.* If the bentonite lies on top of the dry glaze batch, when water is added the bentonite will float to the top of the glaze and become a sticky mass. At this point, the bentonite cannot be mixed into the wet glaze and will clog the screen.

7. BORAX

Borax is a very high fluxing agent in low-fire glazes. Since it is water-soluble, care must be taken when water is added to the glaze batch. *When storing a glaze with borax, make sure you have a tight cover on the glaze container.* If the water in the glaze is allowed to evaporate, you also lose the borax out of the glaze. By adding more water, you start to lose the borax and soon the glaze will not work.

David Cox. Untitled sculpture. Slab construction, unglazed stoneware. Mounted on stained red cedar wood. Gas reduction firing C/9. Height 24", width 8", thickness 5".

Types of Kilns

ELECTRIC KILNS

An electric kiln is the easiest to install. It can be used inside your studio, but electrical connections must be adequate for power supply when the kiln is fired. All electric kilns are rated according to their maximum firing temperature. It is best to purchase an electric kiln with a higher temperature rating than you expect to use. A C/6 (2232°F) or C/9 (2336°F) kiln gives you greater flexibility to fire at higher temperatures. A kiln with a C/04 (1940°F) rating is very limited.

Firing at C/6 or C/9 requires a special 220-volt outlet and a 50-ampere capacity (Figs. 7-1 through 7-5). These higher-firing kilns are more expensive, but are also better insulated, and the Kanthal wiring in these kilns will last longer than that of a low-fire C/04 kiln with nickel-nichrome elements.

The nickel-nichrome elements tend to expand but they remain elastic and can be forced back into the element recesses if they pop out. Kanthal elements will expand if fired only at low tempera-

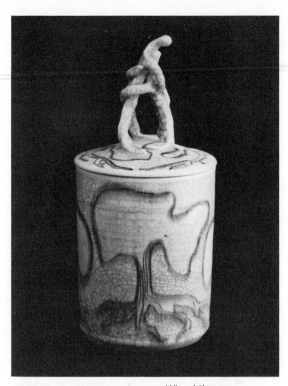

7-1. Author. *Tired Landscape*. Wheel-thrown, porcelain, covered jar. Underglaze on greenware. Crackle glaze overall. Electric firing C/6. Height 10″.

7-2. Author. *Summer-scape*. Slab-construction, porcelain tree forms, partially waxed on bisqueware, crackle glaze. Unglazed areas painted with bright poster-paint colors after firing and spray-shellacked for permanence. Three sections set together. Electric firing C/8. Diameter 16″.

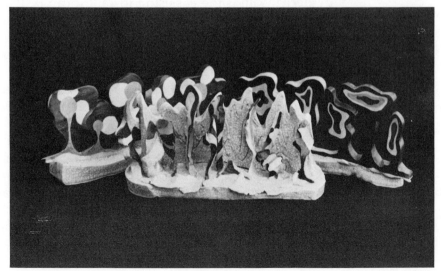

tures. A high-temperature firing is desirable to set them in place. They will become brittle and cannot be moved.

The size of the kiln is also important. Too small a kiln means you must fire more often. A minimum interior size of 18 inches wide by 24 inches deep is necessary to keep from firing too often. If you produce a lot of pots or large ones, then a kiln 24 inches wide by 28 inches deep of 10-cubic-feet capacity should be considered.

A top-loading electric kiln is much less expensive than a front-loading electric kiln. For any size electric kiln, it is advisable to include a kiln sitter, factory-installed. This kiln sitter will allow the kiln to turn itself off automatically when the present temperature is reached. The additional cost is well worth it. Once the kiln is turned on high heat you can leave it alone.

7-3. Author. *Skateboard-scape.* Slab construction, added porcelain figures. Underglaze on greenware, crackle glaze overall, inked to bring out crackle. Electric firing C/6. Diameter 14".

All electric kilns are extremely fragile. The interior lining is constructed of soft insulating brick. With the top-loading kiln, do not lean on the top layer of brick when loading or unloading or you may break the insulating brick. The brick is soft, but with care, the kiln can last for years.

The electric elements can be easily replaced if one goes bad. If an electric element does not work, check carefully to see if there is a break in the element which prevents contact. This is sometimes due to an iron particle in the insulating brick making contact with the element and thus breaking the wire. Dig the iron particle out of the soft brick. Cut a piece of Kanthal wire about 1½ inches long and make a U shape. Using a pair of pliers, interlock both sides of the

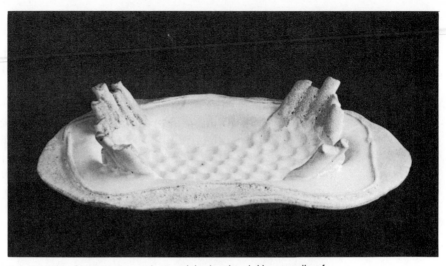

7-4. Author. Slab-constructed, porcelain, low bowl. Heavy coils of clay added. Porcelain slip with silicon carbide around rim. Mat glaze overall. Electric firing C/8.

broken element and push the Kanthal wire into the soft brick. This will cross contact the element and allow the current to flow again temporarily. This saves replacing the element, which will eventually become necessary.

For proper installation and ventilation, an electric kiln should be placed (1) on the stand that comes with the kiln, (2) on a concrete or fireproof floor, and (3) at least 12 inches from any wall.

7-5. Author. Wheel-thrown porcelain bottles. *Left:* Underglaze design applied to greenware, then fired. *Right:* Underglaze wash. *Both:* Transparent glaze overall. Electric firing C/6. Height 6".

GAS KILNS

Gas-fired kilns generally range in size from 10-cubic-feet to 80-cubic-feet interior capacity and should be capable of firing anywhere from a low of C/06 (1830°F) to a high of C/10 (2381°F). Either propane or natural gas can be used. The kiln, because of its rugged construction, can be installed outdoors, with a shed-like roof to protect it from the weather in mild climates. The kiln must be completely enclosed in severe winter climates. It can be constructed or purchased. There are good books on kiln construction listed in the bibliography.

There is no one way to construct a gas kiln, but there are general points applicable to any gas kiln. A firm concrete base is necessary to support the weight of a gas kiln. The correct relationship between the interior size of the kiln and the Btu output of the burners is critical to induce adequate temperature in the kiln. The gas line must have enough pressure for the burners to operate properly. The *stack*, or *chimney*, must be high enough to create sufficient upward draft; however, if it is too high, the heat is drawn up the stack too quickly, which leads to heat loss in the kiln.

Building a gas kiln is an adventure, with the actual firing becoming the final criterion of success.

RAKU KILNS

Raku kilns are the easiest and simplest kilns to build. The fuel is generally propane (bottled gas) or natural gas. The firing temperature is low, not above a bisque temperature of C/08 (1751°F) or C/06 (1830°F). Usually a size of about 30 inches square is sufficient. The object is to get to temperature as fast as possible. This fast attainment of temperature is the reverse of the desirable procedure in firing either electric or large gas kilns. One burner with a squirrel-cage blower can accomplish a firing in 20 to 30 minutes.

The kiln can be constructed of loose hard or soft insulating bricks stacked on one another, or the entire kiln can be constructed of 1-inch kaolin blanket material, light enough in weight that the entire kiln can be set over the pots and taken off after the firing by two people using asbestos gloves. Refer to the bibliography in the back of this book.

7-6. Wayne Higby. *White Mesa*. Landscape storage jar. Earthenware clay, handbuilt with inlaid clay coils, Raku-fired. Glazed, fired about C/06. Height 13″, width 13″.

Joan Weissman. Slab porcelain teapot. Front center of slab cut out. Colored clays laid together, then backed with solid clay slab. When slab stiffened, all slabs put together to form pot. After bisque firing, cobalt oxide thinly washed over surface and sponged off, filling the thin line joints and light sgraffito lines with blue. Colored clay areas unglazed. Transparent glaze over rest of pot. Electric firing C/9. Height 10″, width 10″.

8

Firing Your Pots

PYROMETRIC CONES

Pyrometric cones are used to indicate the firing temperature in the kiln. They are made of a composition of clays and fluxes that will bend at specific temperatures during the firing.

The written symbol of a cone number indicates the temperature at which the cone will bend, showing when the kiln should be turned off. *It is important to use the correct cones for a specific firing.* See Table 8-1 for temperature equivalents of Orton standard pyrometric cones. Cone numbers with a zero in front of the number indicate that the smaller the number, the higher the temperature. For example: C/010 (1641°F), C/06 (1830°F), C/04 (1940°F), C/01 (2079°F). Cone numbers without a zero in front of the number indicate that the higher the number, the higher the temperature: C/1 (2109°F), C/6 (2232°F), C/8 (2336°F), C/10 (2381°F). These temperatures are in Fahrenheit, as noted, not Celsius.

TABLE 8–1 TEMPERATURE EQUIVALENTS FOR ORTON STANDARD PYROMETRIC CONES

CONE NUMBER	LARGE CONES				CONE NUMBER	SMALL CONES	
	60°C	108°F	150°C	270°F		300°C	540°F
022	576°C.	1069°F.	586°C.	1086°F.	022	630°C.*	1165°F.*
021	602	1116	614	1137	021	643	1189
020	625	1157	635	1175	020	666	1231
019	668	1234	683	1261	019	723	1333
018	696	1285	717	1323	018	752	1386
017	727	1341	747	1377	017	784	1443
016	764	1407	792	1458	016	825	1517
015	790	1454	804	1479	015	843	1549
014	834	1533	838	1540	014	870*	1596
013	869	1596	852	1566	013	880*	1615
012	866	1591	884	1623	012	900*	1650
011	886	1627	894	1641	011	915*	1680
†010	887	1629	894	1641	†010	919	1686
09	915	1679	923	1693	09	955	1751
08	945	1733	955	1751	08	983	1801
07	973	1783	984	1803	07	1008	1846
06	991	1816	999	1830	06	1023	1873
05	1031	1888	1046	1915	05	1062	1944
04	1050	1922	1060	1940	04	1098	2008
03	1086	1987	1101	2014	03	1131	2068
02	1101	2014	1120	2048	02	1148	2098
01	1117	2043	1137	2079	01	1178	2152
1	1136	2077	1154	2109	1	1179	2154
2	1142	2088	1162	2124	2	1179	2154
3	1152	2106	1168	2134	3	1196	2185
4	1168	2134	1186	2167	4	1209	2208
5	1177	2151	1196	2185	5	1221	2230
6	1201	2194	1222	2232	6	1255	2291
7	1215	2219	1240	2264	7	1264	2307
8	1236	2257	1263	2305	8	1300	2372
9	1260	2300	1280	2336	9	1317	2403
10	1285	2345	1305	2381	10	1330	2426
11	1294	2361	1315	2399	11	1336	2437
12	1306	2383	1326	2419	12	1355	2471

CONE NUMBER	LARGE CONES				CONE NUMBER	P.C.E. CONES	
	60°C	108°F	150°C	270°F		150°C	270°F
12	1306°C.	2383°F.	1326°C.	2419°F.	12	1337°C.	2439°F.
13	1321	2410	1346	2455	13	1349	2460
14	1388	2530	1366	2491	14	1398	2548
15	1424	2595	1431	2608	15	1430	2606
16	1455	2651	1473	2683	16	1491	2716
17	1477	2691	1485	2705	17	1512	2754
18	1500	2732	1506	2743	18	1522	2772
19	1520	2768	1528	2782	19	1541	2806
20	1542	2808	1549	2820	20	1564	2847
23	1586	2887	1590	2894	23	1605	2921
26	1589	2892	1605	2921	26	1621	2950
27	1614	2937	1627	2961	27	1640	2984
28	1614	2937	1633	2971	28	1646	2995
29	1624	2955	1645	2993	29	1659	3018
30	1636	2977	1654	3009	30	1665	3029
31	1661	3022	1679	3054	31	1683	3061
31½					31½	1699	3090
32	1706	3103	1717	3123	32	1717	3123
32½	1718	3124	1730	3146	32½	1724	3135

(Table 8-1, cont'd.)

| CONE | LARGE CONES | | | | CONE | P.C.E. CONES | |
NUMBER	†60°C	108°F	150°C	270°F	NUMBER	150°C	270°F
33	1732	3150	1741	3166	33	1743	3169
34	1757	3195	1759	3198	34	1763	3205
35	1784	3243	1784	3243	35	1785	3245
36	1798	3268	1796	3265	36	1804	3279
37	ND	ND	ND	ND	37	1820	3308
38	ND	ND	ND	ND	38	1850*	3362
39	ND	ND	ND	ND	39	1865*	3389
40	ND	ND	ND	ND	40	1885*	3425
41	ND	ND	ND	ND	41	1970*	3578
42	ND	ND	ND	ND	42	2015*	3659

* Temperatures approximate. See Note 3. N.D. — not determined.
† Iron-free (white) are made in numbers 010 to 3. The iron-free cones have the same deformation temperatures as the red equivalents when fired at a rate of 60 Centigrade degrees per hour in air.

Notes:

1. The temperature equivalents in this table apply only to Orton Standard Pyrometric Cones, *when heated at the rates indicated, in an air atmosphere.*
2. Temperature Equivalents are given in degrees Centigrade (°C.) and the corresponding degrees Fahrenheit (°F.). The rates of heating shown at the head of each column of temperature equivalents were maintained during the last several hundred degrees of temperature rise.
3. The temperature equivalents were determined at the National Bureau of Standards by H. P. Beerman (See Journal of the American Ceramic Society, Vol. 39, 1956), with the exception of those marked (*).
4. The temperature equivalents are not necessarily those at which cones will deform under firing conditions different from those under which the calibrating determinations were made. For more detailed technical data, please write the Orton Foundation.
5. For reproducible results, care should be taken to insure that the cones are set in a plaque with the bending face at the correct angle of 8° from the vertical, with the cone tips at the correct height above the top of the plaque. (Large Cone 2″; small and P.C.E. cones 15/16″)
6. Permission to reproduce all or any part of this table may be obtained by writing to the Foundation.

Courtesy of THE EDWARD ORTON JR. CERAMIC FOUNDATION, 1445 SUMMIT ST., COLUMBUS, OHIO

The above examples of temperature ratings are for the standard-size cones shown in Figure 8-1. Reading across the chart will give the equivalent small-cone temperatures.

Pyrometric cones are triangular in shape and come in two sizes. The large or standard-size cones are 1¾ inches long; the small or junior size cones are 1⅛ inches long. The cones come in boxes of 50

8-1. Standard pyrometer cones in a bend sequence during firing determine temperature shut-off. Right to left: C/04, C/4, C/9, C/10.

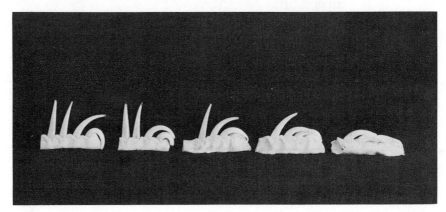

of any one specific cone number. *Be sure to indicate whether standard or junior-size cones are needed.* The following points should be observed.

1. Small or junior-size cones are used only in an electric kiln and only with a kiln sitter. It is important to use only junior-size pyrometric cones in an electric kiln, because there is a temperature difference between standard- and junior-size cones (see Table 8-1). The small triangular cone is set flat on the outside projections of the kiln sitter, while the center projection rests on the top edge of the cone, producing some pressure on it. This pressure will make the cone bend at a specific temperature and automatically cut off the current to the kiln.

   The importance of getting junior-size cones for a kiln sitter in an electric kiln cannot be overemphasized. Only one pyrometric cone is used in an electric kiln with a kiln sitter for either bisque firing or glaze firing.

2. Large or standard-size pyrometric cones are used only in a gas-fired kiln. Here there is no specific cutoff point, and the bending of the pyrometric cones must be watched to determine when the gas to the kiln should be shut off. Even with an external visual pyrometer, which indicates the kiln temperature, cones should be used to check the temperature, as they are more accurate.

The standard-size cones are imbedded in a shallow pad of clay. The bisque fire in a gas kiln only needs 1 or 2 cones, as the bisque temperature is not so critical.

The cones are beveled at the bottom. *Do not set cones in a straight or vertical position. They should be set at a slight angle to help the cone bend on reaching the desired temperature.* When the top of the cone bends in a half circle with the tip touching the cone pad, the prescribed temperature has been reached and the kiln can be turned off.

In high-fire (C/9 to C/10), it is recommended to use at least 4 to 5 cones in a longer cone pad of clay. A series of cones—such as C/04 (low), C/3 to C/6, C/8, C/9, C/10 (high)—is imbedded into the clay pad with C/04 first and C/10 last. *It is important not to get the cones mixed up as they must bend in sequence as the kiln heats up.* Always use two cone pads in the firing, one set at the top part and the other at the lower part of the kiln. This will give you an indication as to whether the firing is even from top to bottom.

Cone pads should always be made up ahead of time to allow the pad to dry thoroughly before using. If a damp cone pad is put into the kiln, there is a possibility it will explode; therefore, *be careful.*

KILN SHELVES

Clay shelves ⅝ inch to 1 inch in thickness are adequate for firing in an electric kiln to C/8 (2305°F).

Gas firing in a reduction atmosphere to C/9 (2336°F) or C/10 (2381°F) requires a different and more expensive type of shelf to withstand the heat and reduction atmosphere. The most common shelf is made of high-temperature silicon carbide in ⅝-inch to ¾-inch thickness. These shelves have become extremely expensive. A substitute for silicon carbide in kiln shelves is a mineral called *cordierite*. In a 1-inch thickness, cordierite shelves can be used in high-temperature gas firing. The price of these shelves is about half that of silicon carbide shelves.

All shelves in gas or electric glaze firing must be coated with 2 or 3 coats of kiln wash before using. Kiln wash can be purchased or easily made. Take a 1-pound container and fill it half full of water. Alternately add a scoop of kaolin and then a scoop of flint. Continue this until the container is full. Put the lid on the container and let the kaolin and flint soak in the water. Then shake the can thoroughly. You should have a thin creamy mixture of kiln wash. If it is too thick, add more water and stir. Two or three thin coats of kiln wash brushed on in a crisscross manner are better than one heavy coat and are less likely to flake off. Use a 2-inch or 3-inch brush for this.

This coating of kiln wash is to protect the shelf in case any glaze runs on to the shelf during firing. It is easy to chip the glaze off the shelf. Periodically recoat the top of the shelves as the kiln wash wears off. *Never coat the edges or the bottoms of the shelves with kiln wash as it will flake off onto the pots on the shelf below.*

LOADING GREENWARE

In the process of loading pots into an electric or gas kiln, the method of supporting the shelves is very important. *Regardless of the shape of the shelves—square, rectangular, or round—use 3 post supports.* The clay post supports should be placed in a triangular pattern under the shelf, not one on each corner. This type of support will result in the least strain on the shelf. It will also give a steady support to a warped shelf and prevent shelves from cracking. *Once the first supports are in place, with the shelf on the posts, all other supports must be placed directly above the lower supports to equalize the pressure of the weight. This method of shelf support is used for all firings in electric or gas kilns.* In electric kilns, always place the cone in the kiln sitter before loading. This is mainly for top-loading kilns. If the kiln is loaded first, it will not be possible to reach into the kiln to put the cone in place.

The unfired greenware pots must be dry before loading the kiln. *If the pot feels cool to the touch, wait another day before firing.* Greenware can be stacked foot to foot, rim to rim. Bowls can be stacked inside each other as long as the foot of the bowl touches the inside bottom of the previous bowl. Any vertical pot can be placed inside another form as long as it rests in the bottom of the piece. *No pot should rest on the inside wall of another pot as the pressure could crack the supporting shape.*

Because pots can be stacked inside each other and on top of each other in bisque firing, many more pieces can be fired than in glaze firing, where no two pots can touch one another.

THE BISQUE FIRING

The procedure for firing greenware is standard for kilns of any size whether gas or electric. All greenware, no matter how dry to the touch, still retains moisture in the clay that must slowly be driven out by gradual slow heating of the kiln. *The low heat is necessary for the first 2 hours, with the door of the kiln propped open 2 or 3 inches so that the moisture can also be driven out of the kiln.* This timing is sufficient for most electric kilns of up to a 10-cubic-feet capacity. *Larger gas kilns of 20- to 60-cubic-feet capacity should have up to 4 hours of heat at low temperatures with the door partially open. The gas flame, even at its lowest output, tends to increase the temperature faster than the low control on an electric kiln. Greater care must be taken to see that the temperature does not rise too quickly, or the greenware might break.* Thick-walled sculptural forms must be heated more slowly with the door open. It takes longer for the heat to penetrate through the clay and for the water to be drawn out to the surface. It is better to use caution and leave the door open another hour or two.

After the initial heating, the door can be closed and the temperature slowly raised. Once a red glow can be seen in the kiln, the temperature can be advanced more rapidly.

Bisque firing should take a minimum of 6 hours for kilns of up to 10-cubic-feet capacity. Larger gas kilns require 8 to 10 hours of firing time after the door has been closed because of the larger volume which has to be heated.

The temperature for a bisque fire should be between C/08 (1751°F) and C/06 (1830°F). Earthenware, stoneware, or porcelain greenware can all be bisque-fired in this temperature range. The clay must be fired at a high enough temperature but remain porous enough to accept a glaze.

After the bisque fire is complete, make it a rule not to open the kiln until the following day. *Never open the kiln if there is any red glow showing. Once the interior of the kiln is black (temperature down to 400°F), it is safe to crack the kiln open 2 or 3 inches. After several hours of slow cooling, it is safe to open the kiln and take out the bisque-fired pots with asbestos gloves.*

THE GLAZE FIRING

1. LOADING GLAZED POTS

This must be done with care. *Double-check to see that there is no glaze on the bottom of the pot, and no glaze at least ¼ inch from the bottom.* The bottom should have been waxed before glazing, and any glaze sticking to the pot should be wiped away with a damp sponge.

Check to see if the shelves need another coat of kiln wash before loading. Chip off any glaze on the shelf from a previous firing. Covers should be fired on the pot, so check to see that there is no glaze where the cover touches the pot (Fig. 8-2). This area should have been waxed before glazing and well sponged so that there is no sign of glaze that could cause the cover to stick to the pot.

8-2. Author. *Diving Off a Dog-eared Dog into the Landscape.* Wheel-thrown porcelain. Added clay figure. Underglaze decoration on greenware. Bisqued transparent glaze overall. Electric firing C/8. Height 16″.

When handling the raw glazed pot, *do not hold the edge of the glazed piece because this will cause the glaze to chip off. Also, do not put freshly glazed pots in any kiln. The glaze should be dry or the sudden heat may make it fall off the pot.* Place pieces close to each other but do not allow them to touch or else they will be glazed to each other.

2. FIRING GLAZED POTS IN ELECTRIC KILNS

This firing will give an oxidation atmosphere during firing (Figs. 8-3 through 8-5). *Generally the electric kiln has a tendency to be cooler at the bottom during firing. To compensate for this, keep the lower switches*

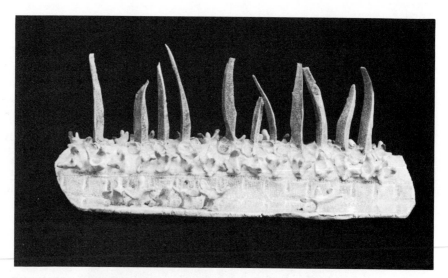

8-3. Author. *Spring Forest.* Porcelain slab construction.
Underglazes painted on greenware, bisqued, crackle glaze overall.
Electric firing C/6. Length 18″.

at a higher temperature setting, increasing the heat hourly. After the lower switches have been on high for an hour, advance the upper switches to high and let the kiln fire off. Let the kiln cool slowly for a day. At no time open the kiln if there is any indication of red heat! Upon opening, crack the door 2 or 3 inches, allowing a slow cooling for 4 or 5 hours. *This slow cooling is necessary to prevent cold air from rushing into the kiln. Since all glazes are glass compositions, the glaze surface will crack if the pots are too hot when taken out.*

8-4. Lissa Paak. *Sugar Babies*. White stoneware, slab construction, added clay. Underglazes and transparent glaze overall. Electric firing C/6. Height 14″.

8-5. Author. *Winter-scape*. Slab construction, white stoneware, black underglaze and crackle glaze overall. Electric firing C/6. Diameter 18″.

3. FIRING GLAZED POTS IN A GAS KILN
IN A REDUCTION ATMOSPHERE

Reduction firing is more complicated than firing pots in an electric kiln, but once the theory of reduction is understood, the beginning potter should have no great trouble with this type of firing in a gas kiln.

Reduction firing basically means that during part of the firing cycle, there is not enough oxygen to burn up all the fuel. The result is that black, smoky carbon in the kiln is "hungry" for oxygen and reduces the oxygen content of the coloring oxides in the clay body and some glazes, thus changing their color. In a gas kiln using forced air, this smoky atmosphere is brought about by cutting back on the air, while in a natural-draft kiln, the flue damper is closed partially so that less air is drawn into the kiln.

In both types of kiln, this cutting back of the air causes an imbalance of the air and gas ratio, resulting in a yellow flame which produces the smoky atmosphere. Checking the amount of reduction in the kiln is a visual task. There should be a yellow flame coming out of the chimney in an updraft gas kiln. In a downdraft kiln, the yellow flame can be seen at the flue damper before the flame goes up the chimney. Also, when the peephole plugs are taken out, the yellow flame should shoot out about 6 to 10 inches. *Be careful not to have your face close to the peephole when removing the plugs. Also, always wear heavy asbestos gloves to prevent fingers from burning.* If black smoke pours out of the chimney and between the bricks of the kiln, the reduction is too heavy. Slightly increase the air or open the damper to decrease the reduction. An overheavy reduction can cause the pot surface to blister or form a black core containing trapped carbon in the wall, and the clay pot will become brittle.

In going through a firing cycle to high temperatures between C/9 (2336°F) and C/10 (2381°F), the creation of the reduction atmosphere is not a continuous process. *If you have an optical pyrometer attached to the kiln to give a visual indication of the temperature rise in the kiln, do not trust it for accuracy, especially at the higher temperatures at the end of the firing. The optical pyrometer is notorious for over- or underheat indications.* Set a pad of pyrometer cones in front of the peephole (top and bottom) of the kiln. Put the cone pads in the kiln at an angle in front of the peephole. Have the lowest cones facing the rear of the kiln, with the highest cones closest to the peephole. During the firing it is easy to see farther into the kiln at low temperatures to watch the cones start to bend. At the end of the firing, the high heat obscures the cones, so C/9 or C/10 should be closest to the peephole. If you cannot see the cones, *carefully blow sharply into the peephole to clear the atmosphere and make it easier to see the cones. Also use welder's goggles or dark sunglasses to more easily see the cones and cut down on eyestrain.*

At high-temperature firing, more cones are used to give a visual correlation of heat between the top and bottom temperatures of the kiln. The following cones should be used: C/04 (low), C/3, C/6, C/8, C/9, C/10 (high) (see Table 8-1). Always use one cone past the temperature at which you are firing to indicate any overfiring. *Cone pads should always be made ahead of time to ensure that they are completely dry before firing. A damp cone pad might explode in the kiln during firing.* Even when the cone pad is dry, start the kiln at a low heat to allow the raw clay of the cone pad to heat up slowly.

The initial firing requires an equal mixture of gas and air to give a blue flame. This is an oxidizing flame, to be continued until the lowest cone bends. At this point, a reduction atmosphere is induced to do a clay body reduction while the clay is still porous. Partial closing of the damper is necessary to keep the reduction atmosphere in the kiln. *This body reduction is most effective on clays containing iron.* From the pink color of the bisqueware, the body changes to a color ranging from orange to dark brown, depending on the amount of iron in the clay body. White clay bodies are little affected by reduction. They will turn off-white to light gray, but no warm brown tones will result. The timing of the reduction can vary from 15 minutes to 30 minutes, depending on the amount of reduction in kilns of the particular size and type used. A lighter reduction can prolong the reduction firing with less danger of trapping carbon in the clay wall.

After the initial body reduction has been accomplished, adjust the gas/air ratio to again provide an oxidizing atmosphere and open the damper. At this point, try to adjust the damper to partially open to maintain a cloudy atmosphere in the kiln, or slightly vary the gas/air ratio. This is tricky, but if you can maintain this cloudy atmosphere, you will have a neutral fire, which will cause a short flame to come out of the peephole. This flame will have a green tip. No smoke should be coming out of the kiln at this time. This neutral flame, after reduction, corresponds to mostly an oxidizing atmosphere in the kiln with a very slight reduction, visible only by the green-tipped flame when you remove the peephole plug. *It is easier to see this color change of the flame at night than during the day.* Maintain this neutral, cloudy condition throughout the firing. It will not interfere with the temperture rise in the kiln. When maximum temperature is reached, introduce another reduction for the glaze, which is now melted on the pot. The timing of this reduction will vary from 10 to 20 minutes depending on how heavy it is. A lighter reduction for a longer time is advisable. At this time the iron in the clay body will interact and break through the molten glaze, giving an interesting spotted effect.

Most glazes are not directly affected by the carbon atmosphere except by giving a smoother, more buttery surface, which is characteristic of a reduction glaze (Figs. 8-6, 8-7B).

Glazes most affected by reduction are those having iron or copper oxides in the glaze. The iron oxide glazes are called *celadon* glazes and the ones with copper oxide are called *copper-red glazes*. The reduction of these glazes changes the coloring oxides from an oxide to a metallic form. The smoky atmosphere attacks and removes oxygen from these oxides, changing the iron oxide color from brown to a soft jade green. The normal green from copper oxide becomes a color ranging from mottled blue-green to strawberry red, depending on the amount of reduction, thickness of the glaze, and type of glaze.

After the final reduction of this firing sequence, clear the kiln atmosphere by returning to an oxidizing atmosphere for 3 to 5 minutes. Then turn off the kiln, close the dampers, and allow the kiln to cool slowly. *Do not open the kiln until the temperature drops below 500°F! The interior of the kiln should be black. Only crack the door*

8-6. Author. Wheel-thrown, white stoneware, small bottles. Overlapping glaze. Gas reduction firing C/9. Height 4".

8-7. Author. *Easter Egg*. Wheel-thrown red stoneware. Two pieces put together. Bisqueware waxed and glazed. Unglazed areas painted with silver and gold model-car enamels after firing. Gas reduction firing C/9. Height 20".

open an inch or two and let the kiln cool to room temperature before removing the pots.

A chemical change occurs in the clay body as the temperature rises and a reverse change occurs as the kiln cools down. This is the reason for a slow beginning firing and a slow cooling cycle, at any firing temperature, to prevent the pots from cracking. *Do not become impatient and take the glazed pots out too soon!*

In reduction firing it is important to keep an accurate written record of each firing, the length of each reduction, and the total firing time. This will allow you to make changes in firing schedules and length or density of reductions based on visual observation of the glazed pots as you take them out of the kiln. With each firing you will become more secure in knowing how your kiln operates. A record of 10 firings should give you complete confidence in your control over the firing cycle and assurance as to your results.

8-8. Author. Wheel-thrown red stoneware covered jar. Animal forms added to surface. After bisque firing, animals waxed, then black glaze poured overall. Animals painted with gold and silver model-car enamels after firing. Gas reduction firing C/9. Height 10".

4. RAKU FIRING

Raku firing or *instant pots* is a rapid method of firing a glazed pot in 20 to 30 minutes which gives immediate results (Figs. 8-9, 8-10).

The Raku clay body can be any clay, earthenware, stoneware, or porcelain containing at least 30% grog. A heavily grogged body is needed to withstand the shock of cooling. Since the firing temperature for a Raku firing is below C/04 (1940°F), the finished pot is still soft and porous. Generally the glazes can be applied thickly, but the glaze should be kept off the bottom of the pot.

The initial first heating of the kiln takes the longest time. While the kiln is heating, place other pots to be fired on top of the kiln to warm them up for the following firing. You can watch the glaze melt on the pot, knowing then it is time to remove the pot from the kiln. Prepare a metal garbage can filled with leaves, wood shavings, or dry sawdust. Have a tight lid for the can. Arrange another can full of water.

8-9. Betty Colbert. Raku vase. Slab construction, unglazed. Surface rubbed with oxides in earth reds and grays. Lightly reduced. Diameter 19". *Photograph courtesy of Alberto Mestas.*

8-10. Billie Walters. Raku construction. Vertical slabs cut, shaped. Pot forms made in a sling. Bisque-fired, then Raku-fired and reduced in leaves and sawdust for variation in color. No glaze. Length 8', width 4', height from 8" to 18".

Since the kiln is immediately opened, a lot of heat is generated. *Wearing a long-sleeved shirt, long pants, shoes, and long asbestos gloves, remove the glowing pot from the kiln with long metal tongs. Place the pot directly into the can of leaves. Cover the can tightly.* A dense smoky reducing atmosphere will be immediately produced in the can (Figs. 8-11A,B, 8-12, 8-13). Unglazed portions of the pot will turn black from the reduction, and lusters and copper reds and golds will materialize from the heavy reduction. After about 5 to 10 minutes, remove the pot and slowly submerge it in water. *This*

8-11A. Cecily Colbert. Raku sculptural form. Slab and coil built. Surface burnished. Heavy reduction to induce black smoked surface. Unglazed. Height 16".

8-11B. Side view of 8-11A.

8-12. Karen Fabricious. Raku vase. Slab-rolled construction. Oxides rubbed into top surface. Lower body burnished. Total form smoked black. Unglazed. Height 7".

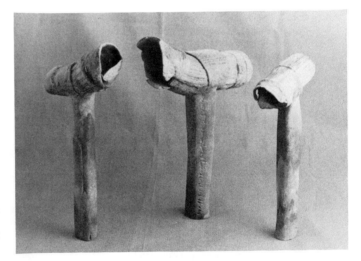

8-13. Karen Fabricious. Raku forms. Slab construction rolled thin with surface impressions imbedded into greenware. Slight reduction, unglazed. Height 10" to 12".

water cooling is only necessary to keep luster colors intact (Fig. 8-14). *Air cooling them may cause the luster to lose its brilliance.* Other glaze colors can be air-cooled. *To get a good crackle surface, put the pot in water. White glazes work well and the crackle is easily seen.* Sometimes carbon forms a thin film on the glaze (Fig. 8-15). Gently wash the surface with soap and water to reveal the true color of the glaze.

This is an exciting firing process. Do not be disappointed if pieces crack and break in the beginning. A high casualty rate is a part of the process of Raku firing and heightens the sense of adventure.

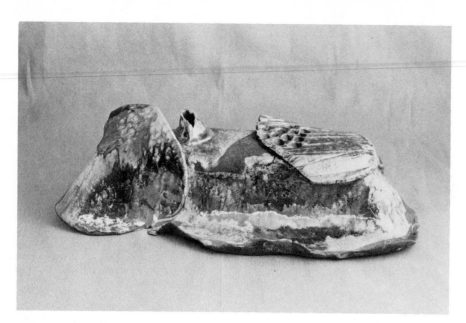

8-14. James Deaton. Raku form. Slab construction. Metallic copper-red glaze. After reduction, immersed in water to retain metallic copper-reds, greens, and gold. Length 18″.

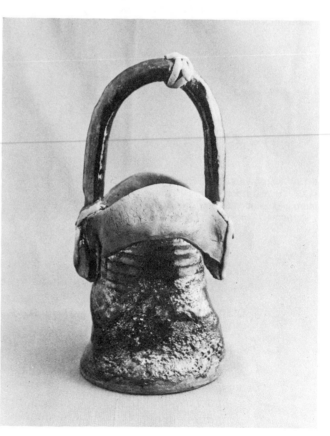

8-15. Sandra Daulton. Raku basket. Thrown base, hollow coil handle, clay slabs added. Partially glazed with unglazed areas smoked black. Height 13″.

8-16. Author. Wheel-thrown, red stoneware bowl with added figures. Brown glass glaze poured in center. Glaze waxed, white gloss glaze poured over bowl and figures. Gas reduction firing C/9. Width 16″.

David Joy. Ceramic teapot. Wheel-thrown
white stoneware, slab-tube handle.
Transparent glaze. Gas reduction firing C/5.
Height 12″, width 6″.

9

Basic Needs for a Small Studio

SPACE

A potter's studio can never be too large but it can be too small. It is best to keep the studio separated from the rest of the house if one is working at home. Good cross-ventilation and minimum direct sunlight allow the pots to dry slowly. Since clay is dusty and messy, it is always necessary to keep a clean studio and to have a place for raw materials, tools, greenware, bisqueware, and glazed ware. It is helpful to have a drain in the floor and, if possible, to hose the floor periodically. Remember that a drain in the floor means the floor cannot be flat; it must allow the water to flow into the drain. If the floor is flat, forget the drain!

A minimum of 225 square feet, whether square or rectangular, are necessary as a working area. Adjustable shelves should be utilized on every available wall for storage, tools, and pots. The shelves and supports should be sturdy to handle storage.

A counter top at least 24 inches to 30 inches deep, wall to wall, allows for a good working area. Beneath the counter top have built-in deep drawers 6 inches to 8 inches in depth, in which up to 25 pounds of glaze materials can be stored. This type of storage makes it possible to get these supplies out of the way.

A storage unit about 18 inches deep, 6 feet high, and 30 inches wide, with doors, can serve as a damp box in which to keep unfinished greenware from drying out. This cabinet can be metal or wood.

Utilize all wall space but keep the center area of the room clear. Here a heavy table about 48 inches square can be used for a clay wedging and work area.

Have two regular electrical outlets on each wall for convenience. This is easy if the studio area is to be newly built. The work space will accommodate one electric kiln. Plan carefully where you want a 220-volt, 50-ampere receptacle for the kiln plug-in. The electric kiln must stand 12 inches from any wall, so it does take up a lot of space.

A water supply is very necessary. If a sink is installed, it must have a clay trap beneath the sink in order to catch any liquid clay before the water from the sink runs into the main pipes. *If there is no trap, eventually the clay from washing tools and pans will clog the main pipes, causing a backup and flooding the studio.* This can lead to an expensive cleanout of the pipes. *An inexpensive deep fiber sink is available.*

The alternative to having a sink is to have two 30-gallon metal or plastic garbage cans filled two-thirds full with water. Tools and pans can be rinsed free of clay in one can, then further cleaned in the other can. This eliminates any need for a cleanup sink.

EQUIPMENT

Kilns and a potter's wheel are the most expensive pieces of equipment needed in a studio. Once purchased, they will last for years with care and minimum maintenance.

1. KILNS

The electric kiln is easiest to install and can easily be used inside the studio. Placing an electric kiln outdoors is not recommended unless it can be completely enclosed with no chance of rain or snow getting near it.

The gas kiln, as mentioned earlier, should be located outside the studio because: (1) it generates too much heat, (2) it needs a stack for draft, (3) it requires hard-to-make gas connections and (4) it would be a fire hazard inside unless it is thoroughly protected from existing walls.

The decision whether to have an electric kiln, a gas kiln, or both depends on your location and firing needs.

2. AN ELECTRIC POTTER'S WHEEL

A good electric wheel is compact, easy to store away, and readily portable. A cheap potter's wheel is a waste of money. There are many brands of potter's wheels on the market today. Sometimes a ceramic supply store will have a demonstration wheel which you can take home to try out. There are several tests you can make whether at home or in the store:

1. The potter's wheel should have a motor rating of at least ⅓ hp.
2. The electric wheel should have a variable speed from zero to at least 120 rpm. *If the change of speed is only a switch from low to medium to high, do not buy the wheel.* The change of speed is too erratic. A foot-pedal pressure permitting continuously variable speeds ranging from low to high gives much better speed control.
3. Test the variable speed at low and medium by putting your hands on the wheel head and trying to stop the wheel head from turning. If the wheel head stops easily, the pulley system or the motor is too weak. This means that in centering clay, the wheel cannot maintain speed, which causes slippage of the pulley or an underpowered motor.
4. The electric wheel should be heavy, not light in weight. Cheap potter's wheels are usually lightweight and they will move during use.
5. Wheel head sizes vary from 10 inches to 14 inches in diameter. The larger wheel head is more versatile in use for larger and wider clay forms.
6. Most electric wheels have a splash pan around the wheel head. Check to see that the plastic is heavy enough to lean on without bending. Since the plastic splash pan interlocks in two parts, check the interlock system. It should snap together as well as release easily. It is necessary to take off the splash pan when a large bat is attached to the wheel head for trimming a wide pot.

3. THE KICK WHEEL

A kick wheel with a motor is less expensive than an electric potter's wheel, but it takes up much more space in the studio and it is not easily moved. The following points should be noted:

1. Some kick wheels are not comfortable for a short person to operate because the distance between the seat and the flywheel is too great. Check the seat height at lower and higher positions.
2. The additional cost of a factory-installed motor is well worth the price, as it allows you to use full speed when centering the clay and to use the foot kick later as the pot expands in size at lower speeds.
3. The motor should be at least ⅓ hp. Check the method of contact where the motor engages the flywheel. Since this point of contact wears out through friction, it should be easy to replace it.
4. The flywheel at the base should weigh between 100 and 120 pounds. Weight here is necessary for enough momentum so the wheel does not slow down quickly when you apply pressure to the clay.
5. Kick wheels are designed with and without splash pans. I would recommend one that does have a splash pan to catch the water on the clay and stop it from flying in all directions during throwing.
6. The splash pan should be easily removable to allow an oversized bat to be adhered to the wheel head for oversize thrown forms or when trimming.
7. Here, as with the electric wheel, the larger wheel head is recommended.

4. SMALL TOOLS

Small tools needed in the studio include:

1. A 30-mesh sieve to screen glazes when wet.
2. A gram scale that will weigh at least 600 grams of glaze materials. It should be calibrated in 100 grams, 10 grams, and tenths of a gram for accurate measurement.
3. A banding wheel, 10 inches to 12 inches in diameter, allows the pot to be hand-turned when decorating.
4. Various plastic containers with lids for glaze storage.
5. A 20- or 30-gallon plastic garbage can is handy to soak clay scraps, which later can be dried and reused.
6. A 32-ounce mortar and pestle.
7. A fettling knife.
8. A flexible scraper.
9. Several sizes of trimming tools with flat, wire-cutting edges.
10. Several elephant-ear sponges.
11. Several large utility sponges.
12. Several wire-end sculpture tools.
13. A rolling pin.
14. A long needle in a wooden handle.

15. Fine copper or brass flexible wire about 18 inches long, used to cut pots off the wheel.

16. Four or five soft watercolor brushes (round, pointed, etc.) as well as a 1-inch flat-edge brush for decorating.

17. A paddle or two for shaping clay (Figs. 9-1, 9-2).

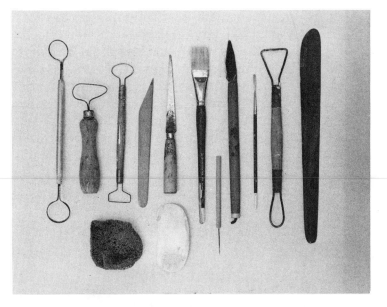

9-1. Ceramic tools.

9-2. Ceramic tools.

With a limited space it is best to buy your clays moist and pugged. It is ready to use with little wedging. Usually the price of moist and dry clay is the same. Moist clay comes in 25-pound blocks, generally 50 pounds to a box. The larger the quantity you buy, the less expensive it is, in amounts up to 1 ton. Storage will decide what amount you can handle at one time. Since the moist clay weight includes water, you lose about 20% of the clay by weight as against purchasing dry clay. To use dry clay means the purchase of a pug mill to produce your own moist, ready-to-use clay. This entails a large expense and a separate clay room for pugging. It is worth the loss of 20% of the clay for the convenience of having it ready to use. Unless you are going into large-scale production, the pug mill is not necessary.

9-3. Author. Wheel-thrown, red stoneware sculptural form. Shapes stacked. Off-white glaze sprayed overall. Gas reduction firing C/9. Height 30".

Maurice Grossman. *Spirit Vessel.*
Earthenware clay. Coil and slab built, pit-fired
Raku. Firing at about C/08. Height 15″,
width 9″.

10

Glaze Formulas

RAKU GLAZES C/010 to C/06

1. *Transparent*

Gerstley borate (colemanite)	80.0	Runny—can be applied thinly over bisqueware. Oxides can be added for color.
Nepheline syenite	20.0	
	100.0	

2. *Waxy Mat*

Gerstley borate (colemanite)	50.0	Apply heavily for a good crackle. Oxides can be added for color.
EPK (Florida kaolin)	33.3	
Flint	16.7	
	100.0	

3. *Glass Red*

Gerstley borate (colemanite)	50.0	Apply heavily. Bright metallic luster. Cool in water to retain luster after reducing.
Borax	50.0	
	100.0	

| Red copper oxide | 10% |
| Black copper oxide | 5% |

When using red copper oxide, mix the oxide in a solution of soapy water before adding it to the glaze. Without the soap, the red copper oxide will not mix with water.

4. *Pearl Gray*

Gerstley borate (colemanite)	50.0
Borax	50.0
	100.0

Runny, glossy surface.

5. *Rough Lava*

Kaolin	25.0
Flint	12.5
Soda ash	62.5
	100.0

Dry, rough surface.

6. *Waxy Off-white*

Gerstley borate (colemanite)	80.0
Ultrox or Zircopax or Superpax	20.0
	100.0

Apply thickly for crackle surface.

7. *Dry Engobe*

Borax	14.3
EPK (Florida kaolin)	57.1
Flint	28.6
	100.0

Dry, white surface.

Apply thinly.

EARTHENWARE GLAZES C/06 to C/02

1. *Colemanite—Barium Mat C/06 to C/04*

Custer feldspar	38.6
Barium carbonate	10.7
Zinc oxide	4.4
Gerstley borate (colemanite)	33.0
Flint	13.3
	100.0

For black add: 10% Manganese dioxide
5% Black copper oxide

For turquoise add: 5% Copper carbonate

2. *N Glaze Mat C/06*

Ferro frit 3304	90.0	Good with red iron oxide
Rutile	5.0	for browns and mat yellows.
Bentonite	5.0	
	100.0	

Add 10% Ultrox

3. *CCA—Bright Transparent C/06*

White lead	63.0	Oxide colors can be added.
Flint	27.0	
EPK (Florida kaolin)	10.0	
	100.0	

Add 2% bentonite

4. *L.R. Mat C/04*

White lead	60.9	Good off-white glaze.
Custer feldspar	10.7	
EPK (Florida kaolin)	3.5	
Flint	18.7	
Rutile	6.2	
	100.0	

For dark brown metallic glaze add: 2% Black copper oxide
3% Manganese dioxide

5. *Alumina Mat C/04*

White lead	50.4	Add oxide colors to glaze.
Whiting	4.5	
Custer feldspar	33.5	
EPK (Florida kaolin)	11.6	
	100.0	

6. *Rutile Mat C/04 to C/03*

White lead	60.8
Custer feldspar	11.4
EPK (Florida kaolin)	2.5
Flint	19.0
Rutile	6.3
	100.0

For light yellow add: 6% Ultrox

For brown add: 3% Black nickel oxide

7. *Leadless Mat C/04*

Ferro frit 3134	37.4	Oxide colors can be added.
Whiting	10.0	
EPK (Florida kaolin)	19.6	
Flint	33.0	
	100.0	

8. *Colemanite Gloss #1 C/04 to C/03*

Custer feldspar	47.0	Oxide colors can be added.
Gerstley borate (colemanite)	33.0	
Barium carbonate	5.0	
Flint	15.0	
	100.0	

9. *Colemanite Gloss #4 Reduction Fire C/04 to C/03*

Gerstley borate (colemanite)	60.0	Dark brown over red clay.
EPK (Florida kaolin)	20.0	
Burnt umber	20.0	Yellow specks over white slip.
	100.0	

Add 2% bentonite

10. *Black Gloss C/04 to C/03*

Gerstley borate (colemanite)	50.0
Albany slip clay	15.0
Bentonite	2.0
Manganese carbonate	20.0
Red copper oxide	5.0
Cobalt oxide	8.0
	100.0

11. *Levy Gloss C/04 to C/6*

Gerstley borate (colemanite)	28.0	Leadless gloss glaze with a wide firing range. Opaque surface. Do not apply thickly on vertical surface.
Custer feldspar	32.3	
EPK (Florida kaolin)	2.4	
Flint	30.6	Good oxidation or reduction. Use on earthenware and stoneware clays.
Zinc oxide	6.7	
	100.0	

For white add: 3% Rutile
                       1% Red iron oxide

For turquoise add: 2% Black iron oxide
                       1% Black copper oxide

For deep blue add: 2% Cobalt oxide
                       2% Rutile

For tan with blue spots (when applied heavily) add: 4% Black nickel oxide

12. *Leadless Mat #6 C/04*

Ferro frit 3191	37.5	Good mat surface. Add oxides for color.
Whiting	10.0	
EPK (Florida kaolin)	19.5	
Flint	33.0	
	100.0	

STONEWARE GLAZES—ELECTRIC KILN C/6 TO C/8 OXIDATION

1. *Rough Granular Mat C/6*

Cryolite	45.5	Off-white, crusty surface. When applied thickly, granular surface.
Talc	54.5	
	100.0	

2. *Mat Glaze C/6*

Nepheline syenite	59.9	Good with multiple dippings. Add oxides for color.
Barium carbonate	22.0	
Lithium carbonate	4.4	
Ball clay	7.7	
Flint	6.0	
	100.0	

3. *Bright Transparent C/5 to C/6*

Whiting	10.0	Runny glaze; apply thinly.
Gerstley borate (colemanite)	15.0	
Barium carbonate	10.0	
Talc	5.0	
Nepheline syenite	30.0	
Flint	20.0	
Lithium carbonate	5.0	
EPK (Florida kaolin)	5.0	
	100.0	

Oxides Added for Color

For white add:	10% Ultrox
For yellow-green add:	5% Red iron oxide
For deep blue add:	1% Cobalt oxide
For mottled tan-blue add:	10% Rutile

4. *Glossy White C/6*

Custer feldspar	45.0	Good glossy base.
Whiting	10.0	Add oxides for color.
Zinc oxide	7.5	
Ball clay	5.0	
EPK (Florida kaolin)	2.5	
Flint	30.0	
	100.0	

5. *Mat Glaze C/6*

Custer feldspar	35.0	Good smooth mat.
Whiting	20.0	
Zinc oxide	10.0	
Talc	15.0	
Ball clay	20.0	
	100.0	

Oxides Added for Color

For tan add:	4% Yellow ochre
For black add:	5% Black copper oxide
For off-white add:	4% Rutile

For lavender add: 5% Manganese dioxide

For light blue add: 1% Cobalt oxide

6. *Bright Gray-Green C/6*

Lithium carbonate	6.0
Nepheline syenite	36.0
Albany slip clay	58.0
	100.0

Add 2% bentonite

7. *K-J Transparent Crackle C/6 to C/8*

Nepheline syenite	40.0	
Flint	20.0	
Whiting	5.0	Good crackle on porcelain.
EPK (Florida kaolin)	10.0	Will not crackle on all clays.
Gerstley borate (colemanite)	25.0	
	100.0	

8. *Glaze VII, Gloss White C/6 to C/8*

Gerstley borate (colemanite)	43.7	Gloss at C/6.
EPK (Florida kaolin)	21.3	Mat at C/8. Try oxide colors.
Flint	35.0	
	100.0	

9. *Tan Gloss C/8*

Albany slip clay	88.5	Good tan. Thick application gives variation of color. Thin application: green. Thick application: black.
Lithium carbonate	11.5	
	100.0	

Add: 8% Ultrox

2% Black copper oxide

2% Cobalt carbonate

10. *Turquoise Mat C/8*

Barium carbonate	25.0	Beautiful color, smooth mat.
Nepheline syenite	56.5	
Ball clay	5.8	
Flint	6.7	
Lithium carbonate	3.0	
Copper carbonate	3.0	
	100.0	

11. *White Mat C/8*

Nepheline syenite	56.6	Excellent base white for colors.
Whiting	12.2	
Zinc oxide	10.8	
EPK (Florida kaolin)	18.8	
Flint	1.6	
	100.0	

For smooth satin black mat add: 2% Cobalt carbonate
5% Manganese dioxide
5% Red iron oxide
3% Black copper oxide

12. *Semi-dry White Mat C/8*

Lithium carbonate	9.0
Magnesium carbonate	10.0
Whiting	10.3
EPK (Florida kaolin)	17.8
Calcined kaolin	7.6
Flint	45.3
	100.0

For strong purple mat add: 1% Black copper oxide

STONEWARE GLAZES FOR GAS REDUCTION FIRING C/9 TO C/10

1. *G.T. Brown-Orange C/9 to C/10*

Nepheline syenite	43.4	Good opaque glaze. Mottled brown. Variation from light to dark with change of thickness.
Whiting	18.3	
EPK (Florida kaolin)	10.3	
Flint	28.0	
	100.0	

Add: 2% Bentonite
2% Rutile

2. *Geff Orange Mat C/9 to C/10*

Custer Feldspar	32.0	Good mat. Does not run. Dark brown when thin, orange-brown when thick.
Dolomite	22.0	
Barium carbonate	22.0	
EPK (Florida kaolin)	15.0	
Flint	9.0	
	100.0	

Add: 1½% Rutile

        4½% Red iron oxide

3. *Slip Glaze C/9 to C/10*

Albany slip clay	60.0	Good gloss glaze. Rich brown to green when thick.
Cornwall stone	25.0	
Whiting	10.0	
Red iron oxide	5.0	
	100.0	

4. *Bleached Albany C/9 to C/10*

Albany slip clay	64.0	Satin mat glaze. Pale yellow-green.
Whiting	20.0	
EPK (Florida kaolin)	16.0	
	100.0	

5. *Golden Brown C/9 to C/10*

Albany slip clay	90.0	Good gloss glaze. Vary color with change of thickness: soft brown to tan.
Dolomite	10.0	
	100.0	

Add 4% Rutile

6. *Black Gloss C/9 to C/10*

Albany slip clay	90.0	Good shiny black. Can be applied to greenware or bisqueware.
Nepheline syenite	4.0	
Cobalt oxide	3.0	
Red iron oxide	3.0	
	100.0	

7. _Lorentzen Blue C/9 to C/10_

Custer feldspar	48.7
Dolomite	12.4
Gerstley borate (colemanite)	6.9
Talc	6.4
Zinc oxide	13.5
Whiting	1.7
EPK (Florida kaolin)	10.4
	100.0

For turquoise add: 1% Cobalt oxide
1% Chromium oxide

Good gloss. Apply heavily for turquoise color.

8. _Bird Mat C/9 to C/10_

Nepheline syenite	71.4
Dolomite	23.8
Ball clay	4.8
	100.0

Add: 2% Bentonite
8% Ultrox

Stiff mat. Good C/10 firing. Color: brown when thin, white mat when thicker. Overthickness turns white mat to high gloss.

9. _Peacock Blue C/10_

Nepheline syenite	56.9
Barium carbonate	38.4
Ball clay	1.3
Lithium carbonate	0.6
Cobalt oxide	2.8
	100.0

Glaze breaks from lavender to purple with heavy application.

10. _Siegal Gloss II C/9 to C/10_

Kona F-4 feldspar	49.0
Fluorspar	4.3
Whiting	9.9
Barium carbonate	6.2
EPK (Florida kaolin)	4.0
Zinc oxide	2.5
Flint	24.1
	100.0

Good gloss glaze. Transparent when thin, milky white when thick. Good with iron wash over glaze.

11. *McVey-Leach Gloss C/9 to C/10 Black*

EPK (Florida kaolin)	10.0	Good gloss. Soft green when
Whiting	20.0	applied thinly; rich blue-black
Flint	30.0	when applied heavily.
Custer feldspar	40.0	
	100.0	

For black add: 1% Cobalt oxide
1% Rutile
3% Red iron oxide

12. *Foster Gloss C/9 to C/10*

Nepheline syenite	82.5	Good gloss. Color break and
Dolomite	8.2	variation from thin to thick
Zinc oxide	2.4	application. Base glaze: white.
EPK (Florida kaolin)	2.6	
Flint	4.3	
	100.0	

13. *Schmidt's Inside White C/9 to C/10*

Custer feldspar	45.0	Good base white glaze; does
Dolomite	20.0	not run.
EPK (Florida kaolin)	10.0	
Ball clay	25.0	
	100.0	

Add 2% Bentonite

14. *Alfred Mat C/9 to C/10*

Nepheline syenite	25.7	Glaze will become glossy if
Dolomite	14.0	slightly overfired. Good effect.
Zinc oxide	22.3	"Buttery" surface when ap-
Whiting	1.0	plied thickly. Mat when thin;
EPK (Florida kaolin)	5.2	gloss when thick.
Flint	31.8	
	100.0	

For tan add:	8% Rutile
For powder blue add:	4% Rutile
	1% Cobalt carbonate
For soft tan add:	5% Red iron oxide

15. *Bova #6 Gloss C/9 to C/10*

Custer feldspar	59.3
Dolomite	6.2
Gerstley borate (colemanite)	11.7
Whiting	11.0
Barium carbonate	3.4
EPK (Florida kaolin)	8.4
	100.0

May run if too thick at bottom. Color breaks well over uneven surfaces.

Colors: 8% Rutile — Tan with blue specks.

4% Rutile

2.5% Copper carbonate — Brown mat when thin; blue-green gloss when thick.

16. *Bova #7 Stiff Mat C/9 to C/10*

Nepheline syenite	53.0
Whiting	19.0
EPK (Florida kaolin)	16.2
Talc	11.8
	100.0

Apply heavily to have best colors and glaze surface.

17. *Saturated Iron Gloss C/9 to C/10*

Custer feldspar	39.3
Whiting	15.4
EPK (Florida kaolin)	10.3
Flint	35.0
	100.0

Rich red-brown when thin; red-brown with black specks when thick.

Add 10% Red iron oxide

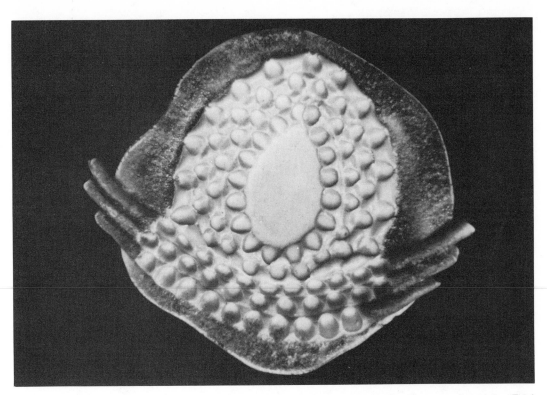

10-1. Author. Slab-constructed, white stoneware, low platter. Thick clay coils added. Porcelain slip with silicon carbide around outer edge. White mat glaze overall. Electric firing C/8. Diameter 16″.

Rex Claussen. *Horse and Rider*. Solid sculpture: modeled, cut, hollowed out, bisque-fired, then Raku-fired with glass-red glaze. Form reassembled and mounted on iron rod embedded in wooden base. Length 14″, height 12″.

Glossary

Albany slip. A natural clay which, when fired to cone 8 and cone 10, fluxes and becomes a brown-black glaze. Its use as a glaze is the primary function of this clay.

Ball clay. An extremely fine-grained plastic clay. Its primary use is as an additive to porcelain and stoneware bodies to increase plasticity.

Banding wheel. A 10- or 12-inch metal or fiber head mounted on a stand. It is hand-revolved to slowly turn pots when decorating them.

Bat. A circle of particle board about 5/8-inch thick. It is adhered to the potter's wheel with clay in order to throw wide, low forms. The bat is taken off the wheel. Later, when the clay bowl stiffens, it can be cut off the bat.

Bentonite. An extremely plastic decomposed volcanic ash which is used to keep glazes in suspension. It is added in the amount of 2% to make clay bodies more plastic.

Bisqueware. Ceramic objects which have had a preliminary firing to harden the body, usually around C/06, prior to glazing.

Burnish. To rub the leather-hard clay with a stone, shell, spoon etc.; to close the pores of the clay and create a smooth, shiny surface. To maintain this surface, the pieces are not fired above cone 06.

Calcine. To heat a ceramic material such as kaolin to about cone 06 in order to drive off chemical moisture. This makes the kaolin more refractory when used in glazes.

Clay. All clay originates from a decomposed granite-type rock which has been exposed to changes in weather and earth movement over thousands of years.

Crawling. The separation of the glaze from the clay body due to excess thickness of glaze or due to a dusty surface.

Crazing. A fine, uneven cracking of the glaze surface due to poor adjustment of glaze to the body or to taking the glazed ware out of the kiln too soon, which results in cold air cracking the glaze.

Crosshatch. A technique of scoring the damp greenware body before adding slip and attaching additional clay forms to the surface of the pot.

Dipping. A process of glazing pottery by immersing the pot in a bucket of glaze. Overlaps of dipping into the glaze create an additional thickness of glaze, resulting in a variation of color.

Earthenware slip. A low-fire clay in liquid form.

Elephant-ear sponge. A flat natural sponge excellent for use when throwing on the potter's wheel.

Engobe. A prepared slip containing clay, feldspar, flint, a flux, and colors. Different formulas of engobes can be applied to dry ware, damp ware, or bisqueware.

Fettling knife. A ceramic knife that tapers to a long, thin, flexible blade to allow easy cutting and minimum clay contact with the blade.

Flexible scraper. A kidney-shaped piece of flexible steel. The scraper also comes in hard rubber and wood. Good for smoothing the inside surface of pots.

Flux. A substance which causes or promotes melting of a glaze.

Foot. The rim or base of a ceramic form.

Frit. A partial or completed glaze that is melted and then re-ground to eliminate the toxic effects of lead or the solubility of borax.

Glaze. A liquid suspension of finely ground minerals that is applied to bisqueware. The ware is fired to a temperature at which the glaze materials will melt together to form a glassy surface on the pot.

Gram. The metric unit of measurement universally used to weigh glaze materials, oxides, and dry slips.

Greenware. Any pottery that has not been fired.

Grog. Clay which has been fired, then ground to various particle sizes. It is used in amounts up to 40% to decrease shrinkage in sculptural forms; in Raku clay bodies to lessen thermal shock: and in throwing bodies to give the clay additional support.

Gum arabic or gum tragacanth. A binder added to the glaze when brushing glazes on the pot is necessary.

Kanthal. A special metal alloy wire used in high-fire electric kilns from cone 6 to cone 9.

Kaolin. A pure white clay used in glazes and clay bodies.

Kiln wash. A protective coating applied to the top of the kiln shelves to keep excess glaze from sticking to the shelf. Equal parts of kaolin and flint mixed with water to a thin creamy consistency give an inexpensive and effective wash.

Leather hard. The condition of raw ceramic ware when most of the moisture has left the body but it is still soft enough to carve, apply slip, add clay, or burnish.

Mat glaze. A smooth, nongloss surface.

Maturity. The condition of the clay, which when fired becomes hard, nonporous; or the point at which the glaze melts and develops a strong bond with the clay body.

Mishima. A decorating technique which involves the process of inlaying a colored slip into an incised line cut in leather-hard clay.

Opacifier. A chemical added to a base glaze to whiten the glaze and change it from translucent to opaque.

Oxides, coloring. Compounds of metals such as iron, nickel, cobalt, chromium, and copper added to glazes, clays, slips and engobes to produce various colors.

Oxidizing fire. A kiln atmoshere which, during firing, contains an equal supply of fuel and oxygen to produce a blue flame.

Porcelain. A hard clay body that is white and translucent when fired to high temperature.

Pyrometric cones. Small triangular cones 1⅛ inches and 2⅝ inches high. They are made of ceramic materials that will bend at specific temperatures.

Raku. A firing process using glazed or unglazed, heavily grogged clay forms which are fired for 20 or 30 minutes, then reduced in leaves and cooled in water.

Reduction fire. A smoky atmosphere in the kiln produced by an unequal mixture of gas and air.

Refractory. All kiln furniture, such as shelves and supports, that is highly resistant to high temperatures.

Sgraffito. A decorative technique which involves cutting through a colored slip- or engobe-covered surface to reveal the clay beneath. This is done at the leather-hard stage.

Shrinkage. During the drying and firing process, the clay shrinks. Firing at cone 9 or cone 10 can involve as much as 15% total shrinkage as the clay particles tighten, making the high-fire ware much harder and durable than that subjected to a lower firing.

Silicon carbide. Particles of silicon carbide, about 60 mesh, can be wedged into clay or put into a slip, then applid to the bisque pot and covered with a mat glaze. On firing between cone 5 and cone 9, the silicon carbide will react with the slip and glaze to produce a rough textural surface.

Slip. Clay in a liquid suspension applied to damp ware to give a contrasting color to the clay body.

Slip combing. The process of trailing a thick slip through a syringe to create a raised slip line on the damp pot, then combing or feathering through the slip pattern to create a wavy, broken linear pattern.

Trimming tool. A tool used primarily to trim leather-hard pots on the wheel. The wire end must be made flat-wire to give a cutting edge when trimming.

Underglaze colors. Commercially prepared stains which are applied under glazes before firing.

Wax resist. A decorative technique of brushing a wax emulsion on greenware or a bisqued pot. Any areas waxed will repel other colorants, slips, or glazes and keep them from adhering.

Wedging. A preparatory technique of kneading plastic clay with the fingers and the heel of the hand in a spiral motion which forces out trapped air pockets and gives a uniform texture. A variation is to cut the clay on a taut wire, then slam it on a canvas-covered table top to force out air pockets.

Author. *Opossum with Babies*. Heavily grogged red stoneware clay. White mat glaze overall. Gas reduction firing C/9. Height 7″, width 14″.

Bibliography

MAGAZINES

American Craft. New York: American Craft Council 10019 (22 West 55th Street). The contemporary related craft scene, craft marketplaces, exhibitions, craft world, where to show, workshops. Six issues a year.

Ceramics Monthly. Columbus, Ohio 43212 (1601 Northwest Blvd., P.O. Box 12448). Covers work of potters throughout the United States, with many articles of interest for the beginning potter. Exhibition dates listed. Ten issues a year.

Studio Potter. Warner, N.H., 03278 (Box 172). Quarterly publication related to the works of studio potters, with articles on all aspects of ceramics.

BOOKS: THE AMERICAN SCENE—
HISTORICAL—CONTEMPORARY

Clark, Garth, *A Century of Ceramics in the United States, 1878–1978*. New York: Dutton, 1979. A cross section of ceramics, well illustrated, showing the progression of ceramic form.

Donhauser, Paul S., *History of American Ceramics*. Dubuque, Iowa: Kendall/Hunt, 1978. Coverage of last 100 years of ceramics with many photographs.

Hall, Julie, *Tradition and Change*. New York: Dutton, 1977. Survey of contemporary ceramics, excellent photographs of leading potters in the United States.

BOOKS: CLAYS, GLAZES, KILNS,
THROWING, HAND BUILDING

Nelson, Glenn, *Ceramics, A Potter's Handbook* (4th ed.). New York: Holt, Rinehart & Winston, 1978. Well illustrated with historical and contemporary ceramics. Text gives a broad coverage of clays, techniques, decorating, glazing, and firing pots.

Olsen, Fredrick L., *The Kiln Book*. Bassett, Calif.: Keramos Books, 1973. A thorough explanation of the processes of kiln building.

Piepenburg, Robert, *Raku Pottery*. New York: Macmillan, 1972. Text on Raku firing process, kiln building, and glazes.

Rhodes, Daniel, *Clay and Glazes for the Potter*. Philadelphia: Chilton, 1970. Thorough discussion of stoneware glazes, chemicals, and stoneware firing. Good reference book for all potters.

————. *Kilns: Design, Construction, and Operation*. Philadelphia: Chilton, 1968. A necessary book when you want to build a gas kiln. Different types of kiln design.

————. *Pottery Form*. Radnor, Pa.: Chilton, 1976. Close-up photographs to help the beginning potter understand forms thrown on the potter's wheel, as well as simple slab construction.

135

Bibliography

Riegger, Hal, *Taku: Art and Technique.* New York: Van Nostrand, 1970. The Raku process and kiln building for this low-fire method of firing.

Woody, Elsbeth S., *Handbuilding Ceramic Forms.* New York: Farrar, Straus & Giroux, 1979. Basic processes and techniques of hand building, plus hand-building approaches of 10 professional ceramicists, with over 350 colors and black-and-white photos.

Index